WORSHIP AS

Faith and Reason in search of a theology of Eucharist

AELRED ARNESEN

Order this book online at www.trafford.com/07-0549
or email orders@trafford.com

Most Trafford titles are also available at major online book retailers.

© Copyright 2008 Aelred Arnesen.

All rights reserved. No part of this publication may be reproduced, stored in a retrieval system, or transmitted, in any form or by any means, electronic, mechanical, photocopying, recording, or otherwise, without the written prior permission of the author.

Note for Librarians: A cataloguing record for this book is available from Library and Archives Canada at www.collectionscanada.ca/amicus/index-e.html

Printed in Victoria, BC, Canada.

ISBN: 978-1-4251-2145-7

We at Trafford believe that it is the responsibility of us all, as both individuals and corporations, to make choices that are environmentally and socially sound. You, in turn, are supporting this responsible conduct each time you purchase a Trafford book, or make use of our publishing services. To find out how you are helping, please visit www.trafford.com/responsiblepublishing.html

Our mission is to efficiently provide the world's finest, most comprehensive book publishing service, enabling every author to experience success. To find out how to publish your book, your way, and have it available worldwide, visit us online at www.trafford.com/10510

www.trafford.com

North America & international
toll-free: 1 888 232 4444 (USA & Canada)
phone: 250 383 6864 ♦ fax: 250 383 6804
email: info@trafford.com

The United Kingdom & Europe
phone: +44 (0)1865 722 113 ♦ local rate: 0845 230 9601
facsimile: +44 (0)1865 722 868 ♦ email: info.uk@trafford.com

10 9 8 7 6 5 4 3

For all who shared in the common life of Ewell Monastery

CONTENTS

Preface i

Introduction iii

1 The Challenge of the Enlightenment 1
   The counter-philosophical drift of the church 14

2 The Quest for the Beauty of Holiness in worship and life 19
   John Wesley 20
   Anglican Evangelicals 22
   The Oxford Movement 26

3 Revelation and Reason 32

4 God - Yesterday and Today 40
   God as Omnipotent 42
   God as Personal 50
   The Biblical 'experience' of God 54

5 The New Testament Perspective 58

6 The Liturgical Movement 67

7	Atonement and the Eucharist	71
	St Mark	72
	St Paul	77
	From the 2nd to the 16th Century	83
	Eucharistic worship and the death of Christ	90
	The Commemoration of Jesus in the Eucharist today	101
8	Remembrance in the Eucharist	106
	Jesus and Remembrance	108
	Theories of remembrance in the liturgy	110
9	Presence	120
	Presence of God	120
	Presence of Jesus the risen Lord	126
	The Presence of Jesus in the Eucharist	131
10	Epiclesis	136
11	Worship as Believing - A Summary	143
Bibliography		149
Index		153

Preface

The title of this book was sparked off from reading Graham Hughes' recent book, Worship as Meaning, subtitled, A Liturgical Theology for Late Modernity.[1] Hughes examines ways of understanding worship. How can Christianity be perceived by society today as having meaning in the 21st century? For the majority who live in this time of disenchantment it is meaningless, at least in the form that the churches portray it. In a dense and interesting book, Hughes seeks to find out what a worshipper today, going in to a strange church, would find meaningful in the gestures, and rites of the service. There is certainly a large question here, as Hughes puts it,

> 'I have wanted to know as well as I could how, in this age of Christian belief, we might make 'sense of' - i.e., draw sense from - the ritual acts of Christians assembled in worship.'[2]

But, as will be seen in what follows, I have felt that while this is a legitimate and in some sense a basic problem, there is a prior need for a clear eyed assessment of the theology of specific main stream areas in Christian worship. There is still, despite the updating in modern language, (striving after meaning?), an underlying, pre-Enlightenment mode of understanding of particular issues which go back 1600 years at least to a tradition which, for various Christian groups, has become the undeviating norm of belief.

I write as one who, at the present time stands outside the regular patterns of parochial worship, but with an experience of 40 years of monastic worship. From this vantage point I stand with all those who also, for whatever reason, stand outside the churches today.

---

[1] Graham Hughes, *Worship as Meaning*, Cambridge, 2003.
[2] ibid. page 8.

From their point of view they cannot see either the sense of Christian faith and discipleship nor the reasons for 'church going' in this 21st century. They have become alienated and disenchanted by all things Christian. For, from their point of view, 'God is no more' in post-modern life and what vestiges remain of the great Christian centuries belong to the past. So I shall be examining particular aspects of worship not as a matter of 'rites' to be observed but as a believing and reasoned response to the risen Lord.

Introduction

It is perhaps not surprising that today there is little enthusiasm among the majority of people in Western and Northern Europe for Christian worship. While the sixteenth century reformation restored common worship in the parishes there came with this reform a recurrence of dogmatic assertions of faith and practice, which today have been eroded by the even greater renewal of thought and science from the mid seventeenth century onwards. As Jonathan Israel writes,

> '[The Renaissance and Reformation in western civilisation] are really only adjustments, modifications to what was essentially still a theologically conceived and ordered regional society, based on hierarchy and ecclesiastical authority, not universality and equality.'[3]

It has taken almost four hundred years for many of us to realise that what happened in the huge shift of understanding in the period between 1650 and 1800, called normally the Enlightenment, has altered our perception of the place of traditional Christian worship in a world changed beyond all recognition from the previous centuries of Christian faith. Israel goes on to write,

> '[The Enlightenment] not only attacked and severed the roots of traditional European culture in the sacred, magic, kingship and hierarchy, secularising all institutions and ideas, but (intellectually and to a degree in practice) effectively demolished all legitimation

---

[3] Jonathan I. Israel, *Radical Enlightenment*, Philosophy and the Making of Modernity 1650-1750, Oxford University Press, 2001[2002] page vi.

of monarchy, aristocracy, woman's subordination to man, ecclesiastical authority and slavery, replacing these with the principles of universality, equality and democracy.[4]

In the first part of the book we need to look back to this explosion of thought and scientific enquiry that began in the seventeenth century and to note the effect this had for religion in Europe. Then, in a brief historical excursus, to note how the Wesleyan, Evangelical and Tractarian revivals of the eighteenth and nineteenth centuries allowed the church to pick up the threads of a traditional theology from the demise of deism in the eighteenth century, which effectively cushioned the church against any radical re-thinking of the theology of Christian worship. Then we shall be discussing the place of revelation today together with our understanding of God. The person of Jesus as the risen Lord as expressed in the New Testament and a brief history of the liturgical movement bring this part to a close.

The main part of the book will be a consideration of four themes that recur in Christian worship - atonement in the Christian Eucharist, remembrance, presence and epiclesis - in the light of the contemporary, reasonable understanding of God, which has already been discussed in the first part of the book. Rarely, if ever, have some of the details of the Christian rites handed down to us in liturgical tradition been considered in the light of any debate about the nature of God. Similarly, the twentieth century has seen the prolific, critical examination of the New Testament but there is a sense, however, that the New Testament conviction that the relationship of the risen Lord to the disciples as the basis of Christian worship, has been by-passed by an uncritical restoration of liturgical ritual understanding. I shall be assessing just how much

---

[4] ibid. page vi.

these liturgical notions, such as the epiclesis, can be today justified in the light of a believable theism and against the background of New Testament presuppositions.

CHAPTER 1

The Challenge of the Enlightenment

It is impossible for us in the 21st century to feel what it was like to belong to seventeenth century society. In England, although the Reformation had changed a great deal of the mediaeval church rites, the biblical narrative as literal fact remained, together with belief in miracles, immortality of the soul and the threat of future punishment in hell. There were certainly isolated deviants throughout the centuries but in this early modern period both state and church would exact the severest penalties.

When Hamlet first sees the ghost of his father and exclaims,

> 'Angels and ministers of grace defend us!
> Be thou a spirit of health or goblin damned,
> Bring with thee airs from heaven or blasts from hell,
> Be thy intents wicked or charitable,
> Thou com'st in such a questionable shape
> That I will speak to thee. I'll call thee Hamlet,
> King, father, royal Dane. O answer me!' - (Hamlet, Act 1, Scene 4)[5]

- we become aware of a climate of semi-religious understanding which is alien to us today. While the reformation, both on the Continent and in England had 'purged' Christianity of what was understood to be un-scriptural ideas of the mass and the whole panoply of papal eccentricities, many of the popular ideas such as angels, spirits good and bad and the understanding of a literal

---

[5] William Shakespeare, *The Complete Works*, General Editors: Stanley Wells and Gary Taylor, Clarendon, 1988, page 660.

heaven and hell remained part of the furniture of society. In fact they were to continue for some long time in the popular mind as superstitions. But the end of the Elizabethan era was to see the beginnings of a more serious reform which has, through the past four centuries, changed how we see the universe, ourselves and nature. For what continued after the reformation in both Catholic and Protestant countries, in universities and schools, was a medieval way of knowledge which went back to the Greek philosopher, Aristotle.

It is even more difficult to comprehend what it was like living under the prevailing tenets of scholastic Aristotelianism by which the world, humanity, nature and God were understood intellectually at that time. Christian theological concepts superimposed on the materialism of Aristotle led to a sort of total theocratic understanding of all that happens in living creatures, of the 'substance' inherent in all things and the motions of the cosmos with the earth at its centre. However, the 'new philosophy' and science, beginning with Descartes, struck the death knell of a system that no longer reflected a reasonable explanation of the world. More than that, as later critics pointed out, the ignorance of how life 'worked' led often to the belief in the occult and magic, demons and spirits. In effect, the medieval scholasticism was unable to do more than describe nature as they saw it, without any possibility of getting beyond what amounted to a purely 'common-sense' understanding. And what they observed were then baldly stated to be so and could not be otherwise.

> 'To have such 'scientific knowledge' of, say, the facts that man is the only animal with a sense of humour, that gold dissolves in aqua regia, or that triangles have angles equal to two right angles, is to know that these things must be so and cannot be

The Challenge of the Enlightenment

otherwise.'[6]

Here we must try to fathom how these pre-moderns, the Christian scholastic philosophers, looked at the reality of life, reducing what they saw to 'substantive forms'. The very term puts us off as it appears to go entirely contrary to our idea of substance as, for instance, when we say that 'the substance was sticky'. But for them, everything that appeared to the senses was catalogued according to its 'substantive form' and 'accidents' or 'qualities'. The form reveals the essential nature of the thing which was defined in terms of its 'quality'. For instance there were properties of 'heaviness', 'colour', 'hotness' and 'coldness'. Once something has been so defined then it was categorically concluded that that was how it must be and there were syllogistic arguments to demonstrate this. So a vast edifice of so-called knowledge was amassed which depended upon arguments without explaining what was the reason for things as they were but merely to re-describe what had been observed. As Moliere said about 'the learned doctors' that they explained the soporific power of opium by referring to its 'dormitive virtue'!

Francis Bacon (1561-1626), a contemporary of Shakespeare, who became Lord Chancellor towards the end of his life, challenged this way of doing science, saying that little time, if any, was given to actual experimental work and the rest of the time was spent, without method, in abstract speculation. Bacon aimed to evolve a new and correct method of research. There is, he said,

> '... but one course left ... - to try the whole thing upon a better plan, and to commence a total reconstruction of sciences, arts, and all human knowledge, raised upon proper foundations ... It

---

[6] R. S. Woolhouse, *The Empiricists*, A History of Western Philosophy:5, OUP, 1988, page 51.

is necessary that a more perfect application of the human mind and intellect be introduced.'[7]

Bacon emphasized that the information we may gather through observation and experience needs to be analyzed by reason and the understanding. He was to be followed later in the 17th century by the eminent mathematician and scientist, Isaac Newton (1642-1727), who echoed the complaints of Bacon and the many eminent philosophers of that century, and noted in the preface to his great work *The Principia*, '[that] the moderns - rejecting substantial forms and occult properties - have undertaken to reduce the phenomena of nature to mathematical laws.'[8] Galileo had already observed this idea of mathematics being the key to understanding nature earlier, in 1623, saying,

> 'Philosophy is written in this grand book, the universe, which stands continually open to our gaze. But the book cannot be understood unless one first learns to comprehend the language and read the characters in which it is written. It is written in the language of mathematics, and its characters are triangles, circles, and other geometric figures without which it is humanly impossible to understand a single word of it; without these one is wandering in a dark labyrinth.'

The 17th century was the cradle of modern science but at the time it was called 'natural philosophy', occupying the minds of all those brilliant men who followed Descartes' beginnings and were critical

---

[7] ibid page 17.

[8] Isaac Newton, Preface to the Reader in the first edition, 1687, of The Principia; in *Newton, Philosophical Writings* edited by Andrew Janiak, CUP, 2004, page 40.

as well as supportive of his theories. It was also a time when this natural philosophy was inextricably bound up with religion both in the churches and in the various governments in England and on the Continent. It was felt that the new ideas were often a threat to revealed religion if not definitely atheistic in tone. Descartes' writings were put on the index of forbidden literature by the Catholic church in 1663, despite the fact that Cartesianism, as it became known, was widely accepted in the universities of Holland for at least a century and a half. It was with Boyle and Newton that these philosophical debates mutated into experimental science in the late 17th and early 18th century. The Royal Society, founded in 1660, for 'The Improving of Natural Knowledge' sought to further the experimental side of the 'new philosophy' and many eminent men of the time, such as Christopher Wren, became members. However, there were those who saw these developments as a concentration on material things to the neglect of the spiritual: 'Men that are much fixed upon matter ... may ... forget that there be such things in the world as Spirits ... and that at last there is a God, and that their souls are immortal.'[9] Yet Boyle defended the growth of experimental philosophy as leading towards spiritual things, discovering the perfections of the Creator. As we shall be seeing, the churches, while accepting the advance of real science through the 19th century definitely bypassed the philosophical questions originally raised by Descartes and others of the 'new philosophy'. We shall just briefly look at some of these questions they raised, bearing in mind that they have not by any means lost any of their challenge for us today in Christian theology.

René Descartes (1596-1650) started out with a clear idea of what

---

[9] Méric Casaubon from *A Letter to Peter du Moulin*, Cambridge, 1669, quoted in R.S. Woolhouse, The Empiricists, page 71.

he felt called to do and in a posthumous paper found in Stockholm after his death there, he vividly expresses his lifelong search for truth:

> 'I shall bring to light the true riches of our souls, opening up to each of us the means whereby we can find within ourselves, without any help from anyone else, all the knowledge we may need for the conduct of life, and the means of using it to acquire all the most abstruse items of knowledge that human reason is capable of possessing.'[10]

For the greater part of his life Descartes was deeply engaged in research into mathematics, optics and meteorology, notably suggesting that natural phenomena could be explained by natural 'laws' of nature. But in the last ten years of his life he turned to writing about what he hoped would be a new system of philosophy to replace the old scholastic style of teaching in the universities and schools.

There were two major questions which Descartes strove to address. First, what can we say about what our senses tell us of things outside of us. Secondly, what is the nature of the 'soul', or the self, in which the mind is active and always, according to Descartes, thinking. Conjoined to both of these was also the fact of God and his relation both to the soul and to the creation. Descartes felt that these were not abstruse matters but could be answered in a simple way for everyone to understand. So he wrote the famous Meditations in the hope that those who read them would follow with him in his patient, meditative discovery of the truth. It is not always realized that Descartes was writing also at a time when there had been quite an incursion of scepticism into European thought

---

[10] Quoted by John Cottingham in *Descartes*, Blackwell, 1988, page 19.

The Challenge of the Enlightenment

from the recently published Latin translation of the Greek sceptic, Sextus Empiricus. The sceptics argued that all our beliefs can be doubted and that all dogmatic claims should be avoided. So Descartes opened his Meditations with a long discussion of how it is possible to doubt everything, even to his own existence,

> 'I will assume that everything I see is false. I believe that, among the things that a deceptive memory represents, nothing ever existed; I have no senses at all; body, shape, extension, motion and place are unreal. Perhaps that is all there is, that there is nothing certain.'[11]

But because he is convinced that God would not deceive him, it appears to Descartes that as he is a 'thinking thing', (or in the later, famous saying *cogito:ergo sum*), then he does exist.[12] Then he comes to the point of realizing that there is in himself the 'idea' of God, something that appears to be innate in himself.

> 'It must absolutely be concluded from the mere fact that I exist and that I have an idea of a most perfect being - that is, of God -

---

[11] René Descartes in *Descartes*, Second Meditation, translated by Desmond M. Clarke, Penguin Classics, 1998, page 23.

[12] John Cottingham points out, ' ... the doubts of the First Meditation are not intended to be as radical as is sometimes supposed. Descartes is not trying to 'validate reason' ... His goal is the more modest one of establishing secure foundations for the sciences, and showing that it is possible, without making any existential presuppositions, to achieve systematic knowledge of the world, what exists.' John Cottingham, *Descartes*, Blackwell, 1986, page 42.

that it is very clearly demonstrated that God also exists.'[13]

Finally, in a long argument with himself Descartes comes to the conclusion that,

> '... once I perceived that God exists and have also understood, at the same time, that everything else depends on him and that he is not a deceiver, I concluded that all those things that I clearly and distinctly perceive are necessarily true.'[14]

While Descartes writes in a very definite way about his understanding of himself and of the world, he is in fact very hypothetical and this is most of all revealed in his absolute distinction between mind and body. Moreover these are both 'substances', as he writes in the Principles of Philosophy:

> 'Extension in length, width and depth constitutes the nature of physical substance, and thought constitutes the nature of thinking substance...Thus, for example, we cannot understand shape except in an extended thing, or motion in an extended space; likewise, we cannot understand imagination, or sensation, or willing except in a thinking thing.'[15]

---

[13] Third Meditation in *René Descartes*, Clarke, 1998, page 42.

[14] ibid. page 56.

[15] ibid. page 132. (Descartes' vision of attaining a true knowledge of the world around him through the use of the intellect appears to depend on first knowing God. It is well known that there is a circular argument here: if the intellect is to be trusted only after knowing God, how can God be truly known by the intellect first of all?)

The Challenge of the Enlightenment 9

However he has to find some form of connection between the body and the incorporeal soul, for while he considers the body as functioning in a mechanical way, there has to be some sort of control through the mind, which turns out to be a sort of system of signals by fluids passing through the pineal gland in the body, in a sort of hydrostatic system, ('prophetically' signaling the present-day understanding of the electrical impulses that control the body's movements!)

While Descartes' theories were immediately criticized by his contemporaries and debated long after his death, they were the result of an insistent desire to penetrate to the reality of life in the world in which our minds are able to reason independently of revelation and to explore how things 'are', rather than just acquiescing in the traditional forms of description and the common resort to 'final causes' of the scholastic philosophers which attributed the behaviour of everything in nature to the benevolent care of God. Descartes attacked those ideas in this graphic paragraph:

> 'It is a common habit of men to suppose that they are the dearest of God's creatures, and that all things are therefore made for their benefit. They think that their own dwelling place, the earth, is of supreme importance, and that it contains everything that exists, and that for its sake everything was created. But what do we know of what God may have created outside the earth, on the stars, and so on?'[16]

Descartes was scrupulously fair in receiving criticisms of his theories which he printed as 'Objections' following on the Meditations. One

---

[16] *Descartes' Conversation with Burman,* translated by John Cottingham, Oxford, 1976, page 36 - quoted in *Descartes,* John Cottingham, Blackwell, 1986, page 97.

of these was Thomas Hobbes (1588-1679) who said that mind is nothing essentially different from the body and that there is no such thing as soul or spirits. Hobbes' ideas were centered round the concepts of matter and motion. Even the perceptions we have of outside things is a matter of motions within the body receiving motions from outside impinging on the eyes. More important perhaps are the criticisms of a French priest, Pierre Gassendi (1592-1655) who rejects Descartes conception that we have innate ideas planted in us from birth. Gassendi argues that everything we know comes from experience in life. As against Descartes, Gassendi also adopts the Greek idea of the atomic structure of matter which was eventually adopted by succeeding philosophers. While Descartes distrusted the evidence of the senses, Gassendi appeals to the fact that observations can be corrected by reason; as for instance when we observe sweat we can reasonably infer that there are pores in the skin which cannot be observed by the eyes alone.

Descartes had another critic who, conceivably, caused the ideas of the new philosophy to spread more widely than might have been the case. It has recently been argued by Jonathan Israel[17] that the fulcrum for change throughout Europe and further afield, must be put at the door of an excommunicated Jew, Spinoza (1632-1677). We do not know why Benedeto de Spinoza was expelled from the synagogue in Amsterdam where he had been living with his family. But his entrance into the philosophical world is clearly a riposte to the received scholastic Aristotelianism of both Catholic and Protestant states in Europe. Shock waves travelled through Europe when it became known that this humble philosopher claimed that God was no supernatural Being, that he was not the creator of the world 'ex nihilo', but was the immanent life-force of Nature and humanity. As against the traditional claims that God was

---

[17] Jonathan I. Israel, *Radical Enlightenment*, Oxford, 2001, Preface, page vi.

The Challenge of the Enlightenment 11

transcendent, omnipotent, omniscient deity, Spinoza claimed to show in his 'Ethics', published after his death in 1677, that while everything was determined by God/Nature, humankind came to believe that what was created was for their benefit, and in their imagination inferred that there was a ruler who should be worshipped, which became a superstition. 'Nature has no end set before it, and all final causes are nothing but human fictions.'[18] The Ethics, dealing with God, the human mind, the emotions, human subjection and human freedom are written entirely in geometrical fashion, giving definitions, axioms, propositions and demonstrations, (like Euclidean geometry), quite distinct from Descartes' almost gentle literary style. But it was entirely in keeping with the mood of the time that mathematics were the clue to knowledge of nature and the universe. It is a tremendously thoughtful work and cannot help but impress the reader (once the format has been mastered!). Spinoza was also a sharp observer of human behaviour, noting in the Ethics, that 'Minds, however, are not conquered by arms, but by love and nobility.'[19] But overall, his writings, which only gradually seeped out, aroused such opposition and hatred for their supposed atheism, that everything in the tussles between the new philosophy and the old traditions throughout the next hundred years, was put down to the influence of 'Spinozism'. Spinoza was well aware that if he allowed his epoch breaking thoughts to be printed during his life-time his life, like many others, would certainly be in danger from the state if not from the churches. His views on miracles, however did get published in his lifetime and were uncompromising. For Spinoza,

---

[18] Ethics, i, 442; Curley, *The Collected Works of Spinoza*, Princeton, 1985.

[19] ibid. page 589.

> '... a miracle, whether in contravention to, or beyond, nature, is a mere absurdity; and, therefore, that what is meant in Scripture by a miracle can only be a work of nature, which surpasses, or is believed to surpass, human comprehension.'[20]

It was to be another hundred years before anyone else challenged the idea of miracle.

Spinoza's idea of 'substance' was at the time quite idiosyncratic, in contrast to the all-pervasive idea of Descartes that only God is the cause of 'movement'. Spinoza formed the opinion that there was 'no such thing as motion, or any motive force external to matter, which to the late seventeenth century mind, was a deeply shocking and revolutionary idea.'[21] So Spinoza formulated the idea that motion is intrinsic to substance, thereby heralding the later discovery of the creation of living and inanimate bodies as a natural process inherent in nature.

Most of the philosophers and scientists who came after Spinoza abhorred his conclusions. But the chase was on to find the basis of the real world out there and how we come to know these facts, and, 'what is knowledge?' Gottfried Leibniz (1646-1716) was one who sided with Descartes' method of analysis, starting from hypotheses. But he proposed, as against Descartes' static understanding of substance as just having the elements of extension, that all units of substance were active, self-sufficient entities which he called 'monads' (from the Greek monas, meaning 'solitary') because they were the basis of individuation in the world. So this theory was bringing into the debate the notion of the reality of force in all

---

[20] Benedict de Spinoza, *A Theologico-Political Treatise*, translated and an introduction by R. H. M. Elwes, Dover Publications, New York, 2004, page 87.

[21] Israel, page 251.

activity that is experienced in every form of life and in the universe. On the other hand, John Locke (1632-1734) was more concerned about how we come to know things. What is knowledge and how do we come by it? His response was 'Knowledge (then) seems to me to be nothing but the perception of the connexion and agreement, or disagreement and repugnancy of any of our ideas.'[22] Locke repudiated the Cartesian idea that knowledge was generally to be considered as innate, for prior to experience the mind is as a blank sheet of paper and he looked for an understanding of the material world to be gained from experience, which gave us 'ideas', instead of simply by postulating a hypothesis. One who sided with Locke to the extent that he held all knowledge could only come from experience was David Hume (1711-1776). But Hume was that much more sceptical than his predecessors, criticising any form of argument from the design of the world to prove a designer,

> ' ... I much doubt whether it be possible for a cause to be known only by its effect (as you have all along supposed) or to be of so singular and particular a nature as to have no parallel and no similarity with any other cause or nature, that has ever fallen under our observation.'[23]

If Leibniz can be called a rationalist, as with Spinoza and Descartes, Locke and Hume could be called 'empiricists'. At least those were the terms used later by Kant (1724-1804) in his aim to bring together arguments from reason with those from observation or

---

[22] John Locke, *An Essay in Human Understanding*, edited by Roger Woolhouse, Penguin, 1997, Book IV, 1:§2. Page 467.
[23] David Hume, *An Enquiry concerning Human Understanding*, in David Hume, Oxford Philosophical texts, edited by Tom L. Beauchamp, Oxford 1999, page 198.

experiment. Kant brought the philosophical enquiry of the previous century and a half to a temporary fulfilment and conclusion, while the work of Isaac Newton in mathematics and optics signalled the true beginning of science as we know it today. Newton was adamant that hypothetical schemes without observation and experiment were of no use. However, Newton was criticised over his work on the law of universal gravitation because he admitted that he had no explanation for gravitation. While he had ruled out a common idea of 'action at a distance', which the new philosophers characterised as 'occult', Newton may have personally thought that God was the cause of gravitation. I shall come back to this concept of 'action at a distance', or as we may say today, 'remote control', later on.

The religious antipathy to all these new discoveries of the mind and of the experimental sciences remained. The churches throughout Europe were distinctly hostile towards all these developments, maintaining that this materialism and the mechanical view of the universe fostered atheism among the population. In fact most of the philosophers, apart from Spinoza, were observant Christians of their respective churches, although it was said of Leibniz that he rarely attended church and Newton had secret doubts about some of the orthodox dogmas of the 4th century. But, as we know, empirical science continued to prosper after Newton and became further and further divorced from the religious establishment in practice.

The counter-philosophical drift of the church

The close of the early Enlightenment period could be said to coincide with Bishop George Berkeley (1685-1783). Berkeley was concerned that there appeared to be too much of a materialist outlook among his predecessors and wished to see philosophy linked more with belief in God the Creator and Provider of the world. He wished to sustain the view that, as he said,

The Challenge of the Enlightenment 15

'the things immediately perceived are ideas which exist only in the mind ...(to which is joined the common-sense view) that those things ...(we) immediately see are the real things.'[24]

This was taken to mean that there is no reality other than minds or spirits and their ideas. His views have been termed 'immaterialist' but he found that his arguments to sustain such a view of the world and of our part in it were ridiculed for their seeming incoherence. So Dr Johnson is said to have begged a Berkeleian not to take his leave from the group that he was with, 'for we may perhaps forget to think of you, and then you will cease to exist.'[25] It is significant that this reversal of Berkeley's predecessors views (although they differed among themselves) came just at this time, at the beginning of the 18th century - (Berkeley's Treatise concerning the Principles of Human Knowledge was published in 1710) - when the Newtonian physics was becoming well known, and a spate of clerical scepticism (in general labelled 'deism') concerning religious things was beginning to surface as a result of the mechanistic views of the scientists. It was against this sceptical attitude that Berkeley aimed to recover a more spiritual understanding

'Deism' was the view that reason does not require revelation and that God as creator and sustainer of the creation does not intervene in the affairs of the world. This was contrary to a specific declaration by Descartes in the Principles that 'we should impress on our memory as a supreme rule that whatever was revealed to us by God should be believed as most certain. ... we should put our faith

---

[24] Quoted in Woolhouse, page 114.

[25] In Boswell's *Life of Johnson*, ed. G. B. Hill (Oxford, 1887) iv.27; quoted in Woolhouse, page 113.

exclusively in divine authority rather than in our own judgement.'[26] While most of the philosophers following Descartes would have agreed with him in this, chiefly it must be said on account of their contemporary situation vis- à-vis the church authorities, Spinoza had already discounted the divine authority of the revelation of Scripture in no uncertain terms, 'admit no principles for interpreting Scripture and discussing its contents save such as they find in Scripture itself ... even as the knowledge of nature is sought from nature.'[27]

We shall need to discuss the problem of reason/revelation later in connection with particular instances. While the French deists, led by Voltaire and Rousseau remained strong throughout the eighteenth century, the English deists did not have a great influence in this country. But whatever the state of religion in England in the middle of the century it is clear that there was no thought that the astonishing energy of the men of the new philosophy in seeking the truth of our situation in the world and universe was about to be applied to accepted, traditional perceptions of the practice of Christianity. The drift away from the churches by ordinary people that lasted well into the nineteenth century, was accompanied by an unspoken assertion by the church that it had God on its side in its assumption that the modern world that was being born had nothing to say to its traditional theological understanding of worship. For instance the ideas of God that had been traditionally held and the possibility of divine action and/or punishment in this world or the next remained firmly fixed in any account of religion, catholic or protestant. However, we need to take notice of the fact that the outcome of the 'new philosophy' helped to create a dichotomy

---

[26] *The Principles of Philosophy*, Part I, §76, quoted in René Descartes, transl. Desmond M. Clarke, Penguin Books, 1998, page 144.

[27] Benedict de Spinoza, *A Theologico-Political Treatise*, transl R. H. M. Elwes, Dover, 2004, page 99.

between the human, spiritual and free life of humankind and the scientific exploration of the universe and of the material world. But as David Jenkins in his Bampton lectures maintains, the new philosophers and scientists were in a desperate situation,

> 'It seemed clear to [thinkers like Descartes and Kant and their successors] that science and technology advance by methods that are necessarily neutral, impersonal and deterministic. It was also clear that if such methods extend exhaustively to everything that can in any sense be said to exist then the essentially human, spiritual and lively aspects of our existence as free, or potentially free persons are done away with. Further, there was no assistance or illumination from theology or from officially Christian thinking to baptize this situation as a whole into an understanding which could see the neutral and deterministic material of science as clearly within a transcendent personal purpose. Rather, the Church fell back on its own sacred realm as over against the powerful growing secular and scientific realm by which it was increasingly threatened.'[28]

At the end of the 18th century the horrors of the Terror unleashed by the French revolution alarmed both state and church in England to the degree that conservatism in politics and religion got a new lease of life. It was not only that the much needed reform of the established church was put on hold[29], but the light of knowledge started by the 17th century new philosophy was left behind, seemingly for ever, as a ship draws away from land. It was certainly

---

[28] David E. Jenkins, *The Glory of Man*, SCM, 1967, pages 68-69. (My emphasis).

[29] See Alec R. Vidler, *The Church in an Age of Revolution*, Penguin, 1961.

true that a rather moribund church needed reform[30] but as we shall see, the religious revivals of the 19th century and the liturgical renewal of the 20th century re-created a pietistic and traditional basis for Christian worship.

---

[30]"No institution was more obviously in need of (reform) than the Established Church. There were glaring abuses and inequalities in its system, that had continued uncorrected since the time of feudalism, and would no longer be tolerated now that the middle classes were winning power. Ibid pages 44-45.

CHAPTER 2

The Quest for the Beauty of Holiness in worship and life

When it is remembered that all through the period of the new philosophy England was going through one of the most terrible phases in its history and that the Continent was racked with inter-state and inter-confessional wars, it is all the more remarkable that what was accomplished has led to the successful establishment both of modern science and social freedom. In England Archbishop Laud (1573-1645) sought to put the clock back ecclesiastically, restoring the altars to the east end and enforcing strict uniformity of worship. His execution in 1645 by order of attainder, brought by the Long Parliament, was followed by the execution of Charles I on 30th January, 1649. The civil war, the eventual Restoration of the monarchy in 1660 and the ejection of presbyterian clergy who would not conform must have been very disturbing for the equilibrium of daily life. The late 18th century was a dangerous time. The French revolution caused both a revulsion of feeling and a conservative reaction throughout Europe. While the forward looking philosophy and science had gained much ground, the situation of whole populations was a breeding ground for revolution. It has been wisely remarked that,

> 'The age of reason had forgotten certain fundamental needs; natural religion might satisfy the minds of some, but the hearts of multitudes were hungry. The weaknesses of the established church - its failure to provide adequate care, the inflexibility of its parish system, its neglect of the new towns - left a vast and needy population waiting to be touched by a new word of power.'[31]

---

[31] G. R. Cragg, *The Church and the Age of Reason*, 1648-1789, Pelican books, 1960 [1966, 1970], page 141.

But despite the turbulence of the times, or because of them, there was a stirring of religion in England, brought about by women and men of great calibre. There is much that is inspiring in these movements we are now going to trace, however briefly. They are important for what they achieved for their times but it is also important to note how it was impossible to break out of the theologically conservative stance of the period. While they revived the spirit of Christianity for many people, especially the poor and those whose worked in the new-found industrial 'factories', there was a renewal of conservative reformation doctrines such as the penal substitutionary theories of the death of Jesus. In the later 19th century there was the different conservative revival of pre-reformation 'catholic' and romantic, Gothic ideals. All these movements contributed to the much later 20th century loss of confidence in out-dated religious language and theology. We need to note all the characteristics of these revivals so that in the later sections of the book we may make the attempt to apply the search for truth about ourselves and the world around us, which the early Enlightenment sparked off, to aspects of our worship.

We might also note that what was remarkable about this period of the revivals, was the hymns that were being sung in an effort to bring participation to congregations in corporate worship. While what appeals to congregations today are the tunes (!), it is important to notice the words for they provided a theology for the 'common folk' that has more than anything provided a subtle background to the understanding of worship in our own time.

John Wesley (1703-1791)

The very remarkable revival brought about by John Wesley in the latter part of the 18th century will always be counted as one of the great Christian movements. In his preaching and care for all sections

The Quest for the Beauty of Holiness in worship and life   21

of a divided society, particularly for the many poor and homeless, Wesley witnessed to the Spirit working in his ministry as few have done throughout Christian history. A child of his times, Wesley wished to be loyal to the Church of England and its liturgy. But it was a pietistic movement and the people who committed themselves to be Methodist, by and large had no real feel for the parish church where there was generally no 'warmth' such as came from the singing of Charles Wesley's hymns. The Established Church for its part had no real sympathy with the emotional style of the movement even though its discipline and commitment was far beyond what obtained in the parish churches of the day. Bishop Butler is said to have rebuked Wesley, saying, 'Sir, the pretending to extraordinary revelations and gifts of the Holy Ghost is a horrid thing - a very horrid thing.' While Wesley's preaching was about the need to repent, he turned away from the Calvinistic doctrine that God admits to salvation only those whom he chooses, while the rest go into everlasting damnation. Wesley insisted, as an Arminian, that God wishes all people to be saved and this comes out in the strongly Christocentric hymns of Charles. Charles' hymns were the Wesleyan movement's 'greatest glory. They explain the power of its appeal, and constitute its most revealing record.'[32] Many are a pure celebration of the gospel, mirroring in accessible verse the words of the New Testament:

> Lives again our glorious King;
> Where, O Death, is now thy sting?
> Dying once, he all doth save;
> Where thy victory, O grave?

Sometimes, however, the Scriptural source, literally accepted, sets a

---

[32] ibid. Cragg, page 149.

problem for today:

LO! He comes with clouds descending,
   Once for favoured sinners slain; ...
   God appears, on earth to reign.

But for the Eucharist, Charles sees to the heart of the New Testament vision:

Author of life divine,
Who hast a table spread,
Furnished with mystic wine
And everlasting bread,
Preserve the life thyself hast given ...

Occasionally there are substitutionary echoes, (following the Markan reference) in:

Victim Divine ...
Thy blood is still our ransom found,
And spreads salvation all around.

One can imagine that it would be hard for one used to singing these verses to feel at home with the monochrome 1662 worship of the parish churches as John Wesley urged his supporters to do. As we know, the break came eventually with the Established Church and the dynamical, Christ centred pietism of a relationship with the living Christ continued as a dissenting approach to worship.

Anglican Evangelicals

In one sense the Anglican Evangelical revival carried on the

The Quest for the Beauty of Holiness in worship and life 23

Methodist revival within the Church of England. 'They were men of the Reformation, who preached the cross, the depravity of man, and justification by faith alone.'[33] Charles Simeon (1759-1836) was one of the most notable evangelicals and there were several eminent men who lived at Clapham in London, known as the Clapham Sect, who with Wilberforce and many others, led the way in the abolition of the slave trade. It was made illegal on 25 March 1807 in the Abolition of the Slave Trade Act to capture or trade in slaves, and finally forbidden in the Slavery Abolition Act of 1833. Simeon and Henry Martyn were instrumental in setting up the Church Missionary Society and the interdenominational British and Foreign Bible Society, both of which did wonderful work through and beyond the nineteenth century.

The social life of the country was in a desperate state and reform both of parliament and church were put back on account of the perceived danger of the effect of the French revolution.

> '... all the poor were conscious of their poverty, of the leaking roofs of their ill-furnished, insanitary homes and of the mortality of their young children ...It was an age of coarseness, political corruption, cruelty and drunkenness.'[34]

In 1835 the Tory government appointed an Ecclesiastical Commission to reform the Church of England. In succeeding years the dioceses were reorganized, pluralism and non-residence were dealt with and cathedral chapters reduced. The evangelical party set themselves behind these much needed reforms. It has been said that

---

[33] Owen Chadwick, *The Victorian Church*, Part 1, Adam & Charles Black, 1966, pages 440-441.

[34] S.C.Carpenter, *Church & People, 1789-1889*, Part I, SPCK, 1959, page 27.

the party

> 'was in tune with, and indeed largely responsible for, the ethical earnestness of the Victorian middle classes. But its theology was narrow and naïve, and partly in reaction from the effects of the Oxford movement it became fanatically anti-Catholic as well as anti-liberal.'[35]

But for the evangelicals, as for Wesley, it has been said that it had also an overbearing concern for reform of the individual soul. This was echoed in many of the hymns of the period, where, for example in Edward Cooper's hymn (1770-1833),

Father of heaven, whose love profound
A ransom for our souls hath found,
Before thy throne we sinners bend:
To us thy pardoning love extend.

- there is the refrain in each verse: Before thy throne we sinners bend.

The idea that Christ suffered the penalty of our sin is often present, as in Mrs Alexander's hymn (1818-1895):

There was no other good enough
To pay the price of sin.
He only could unlock the gate
Of heaven, and let us in.

---

[35] Alec R. Vidler, The Church in an Age of Revolution, Pelican, 1961, page 49.

The Quest for the Beauty of Holiness in worship and life

The wrath of God for those who do not believe is thundered out in Old Testament terms in the hymn by Bishop Walsham How (1823-1897):

'Who is this so weak and helpless ...,
'Tis our God, who gifts and graces
   On his Church now poureth down;
   Who shall smite in holy vengeance
   All his foes beneath his throne.'

Despite the philanthropic work of the evangelical party there is here a sombre, unsmiling and unrelenting judgement made upon humanity on behalf of God. The evangelicals were not noted for their joyousness at the time, their lives being rigorously disciplined and orientated by a literal acceptance of Scripture. It was a time, above all, to attract the people back to church.

> 'Bishop Ryder, the evangelical bishop of Lichfield and Coventry, issued a charge of 1832 lamenting that the churches of the diocese had seating capacity for less than a third of the population, that less than a quarter of these seats were free, that only a quarter of those who attended church were communicants. Analysing the figures, we find that about 2½ per cent of the population of that diocese were communicants.'[36]

The large churches that were built in London during bishop Blomfield's (1786-1857) time to accommodate the rising population, while doubtless useful at the time, are today probably less than full memorials of that too energetic bishop!

---

[36] Owen Chadwick, The Victorian Church, Part I, Adam & Charles Black, 1966, page 333.

The Oxford Movement

The initial concern of the Oxford movement had been about the government's intention to suppress 10 Irish sees. John Keble's assize sermon on July 14th, 1833 challenged this usurpation of ecclesiastical rights. So there emerged the typical concern of the movement to re-instate the idea of the Church as the basis for Christian faith and practice. By this they meant the divine nature of the church, its apostolic ministry and the centrality of sacramental worship. From 1845 when Newman seceded to Rome there was a gradual build up of this concern, particularly among the clergy. It has been said the movement was

> 'narrowly ecclesiastical. The leaders of the movement, good scholars as they were, looked upon scholarship as a useful servant for establishing their ecclesiastical conclusions. They were not interested in philosophy, except in so far as it might become a buttress for orthodox theology.'[37]

From the beginning there had also been a desire to stem the ideas of liberalism in theology. The early nineteenth century saw a swing throughout Europe against the rationalism of the Enlightenment. The Oxford movement in particular

> 'wanted to find a place for the poetic or the aesthetic judgement; their hymnody shared in the feelings and evocations of the romantic poets; they wished to find a place and value for historical tradition, against the irreverent or sacrilegious hands of critical revolutionaries for whom no antiquity was sacred.'[38]

---

[37] ibid, *Victorian Church*, page 111.

[38] Owen Chadwick, *The Mind of the Oxford Movement*, Adam & Charles (continued...)

The Quest for the Beauty of Holiness in worship and life

The romantic movement, which had begun in the late 18th century, popularizing both mediaeval Gothic and a mystical and poetic spirit, flourished at this time. Wordsworth,[39] Coleridge and Southey were the outstanding representatives of the search for a new experience of a freedom of literary and political views to offset the prevailing anxiety of a war-torn civilisation. Stephen Gill, reviewing Wordsworth's views in 1878-9, expresses Wordsworth's reaction to what was seen at the time to be the agnostic or even atheistic sapping of man's inner nature as the result of the age of Reason,

> '... the universe is not mechanical and dead, but alive and vitally connected with the human mind; awakened consciousness leads to an awakened moral sense and must lead to communion with the divine. In the profoundest sense, love of nature leads to love of Man and awareness of God.'[40]

The Cambridge Camden Society, formed in 1839 and led by John Mason Neale, resolved to restore the architecture, decoration and ritual of the mediaeval gothic churches. The members were not Tractarians but rather antiquarian, imbued with the desire to restore 'mystery' in worship. Although the movement was dissolved in 1845

---

[38](...continued)
Black, 1960, page 12.

[39] See Wordsworth's poem, 'The world is too much with us' -
'The world is too much with us; late and soon,
Getting and spending, we lay waste our powers:
Little we see in nature that is ours;
We have given our hearts away, a sordid boon! ...' in *William Wordsworth*, The Major Works, edited by Stephen Gill, Oxford, 2000, page 270.

[40] ibid. page xviii.

after a controversy surrounding their part in restoring the Round Church in Cambridge, complete with a stone altar and credence, its ideals were continued by the Ecclesiological Society of London.

Pusey had assumed the leadership of the movement after Newman's departure and he had always hoped that community life could be restored in the Church of England. This happened in Plymouth in 1848 when Priscilla Sellon began a sisterhood which worked with the victims of cholera and gained the approval of everyone for their selfless service. Another community began at Wantage in the same year and started a school. From these small beginnings came the later communities for both men as well as women in the late nineteenth century. These were always seen as the pinnacle, as it were, of the struggle of the catholic movement to achieve a restoration of pre-Reformation spirituality which they felt had been sorely lost in the break with Rome. Up to the 1930s these communities were often modelled on Roman Catholic communities on the Continent and so their liturgical life had a definite catholic slant which set them apart from many parishes in the church. But during the course of the past century the traditions of these communities strikingly affected the Church of England in many ways, leading to the acceptance of liturgical rites and ceremonial and a theology of liturgy which I shall shortly be discussing.

Some of the characteristic devotion of the movement was expressed in the hymns of the period, as well as in the translation of mediaeval verses from Aquinas. There was an emphasis laid on the presence of Jesus in the sacramental species, as in this translation from the Latin of the 17th century by Athelstan Riley (1858-1945):

'O Jesu, by thee bidden,
We here adore thee, hidden
Neath forms of bread and wine.'

The Quest for the Beauty of Holiness in worship and life

G. H. Bourne's hymn (1840-1925) resonates with less certainties, sung to the well known, noble tune of St Helen:

Here our humblest homage pay we:
Here in loving reverence bow;
Here for Faith's discernment pray we,
Lest we fail to know thee now,
    Alleluya,
Thou art here, we ask not how.

Or in the well known hymn of Francis Stanfield (1835-1914):

'Sweet Sacrament divine,
Hid in thine earthly home,
Lo, round thy lowly shrine,
With suppliant hearts we come;

    In 1903, under archbishop Randall Davidson, a Royal Commission was appointed to look into ecclesiastical discipline on account of the disturbances raised by some of the ritualistic controversies of the later Tractarian supporters. One of the conclusions it came to was that the 1662 Book of Common Prayer was 'too narrow for the religious life of the present generation.' It was about this time that liturgical scholars were becoming acquainted with manuscripts of worship from the early centuries and there began the scholarly and practical work of the liturgical movement on the Continent and in this country. I shall be referring in detail to some aspects of this work later on. Its orientation could be called roughly 'catholic' and in England this was summarised by one writer in the following terms: 'As the Anglican Communion recovers its catholic heritage, the Calendar becomes of increasing importance ..."[41]

While the 20th century saw a great improvement in the state of the fabric of the churches and in the quality of worship, apart from isolated criticisms of the theology that had not changed, there was a widespread idea that what we had in the church was the best sort of traditional, reformed Christian belief. But it has become evident in these early years of the 21st century that there is a great gulf fixed between what is called the secular life of humankind and the practice of Christianity. So there is a sense that the work of the revivalists of the 19th century has fostered a conservative view of Christian faith and worship which cannot be sustained today. We have moved on in the 'updating' of the language of worship but without any real consideration of the theology of worship. While it was true that in the first three centuries the Christian communities set themselves apart from the life around them to a certain extent, this was on account of the pressures exerted on 'illegal' movements by the Roman state. It would be wrong to conclude that they were not at all influenced by other religious movements around them but it was not until the late 4th century that the church became more open to the influences of the world in which it was set to be the religion of the state. Today the case is different. Christian faith needs to be seen as on the one hand a particular faith movement but also seen to be in accord with the accepted knowledge of our human lives and of the world and cosmos around us. Reason has an important part to play in what follows as we consider details of Christian worship and our understanding of God in the 21st century. Above all, it is important how we view the revelation that is in the Scriptures and of our understanding of God. It is to this that we now turn, followed by a necessary review of the presuppositions of the New Testament authors and of the rise of the Liturgical movement in the

---

[41] W. K. Lowther Clarke, *Liturgy and Worship*, SPCK, 1932, page 201.

The Quest for the Beauty of Holiness in worship and life 31

20th century.

CHAPTER 3

Revelation and Reason

The 19th century was a turning point in the debate between the new natural science and the church. While the two sides eventually agreed to go their own way peaceably that did not mean that the church was reconciled to the new knowledge. In April 1892, Bishop Westcott wrote, 'Physicists are beginning, I think, to recognize that they deal only with abstractions, and that such a fact as the Incarnation is alone able to give reality to human knowledge.'[42] In that remark by a very eminent New Testament scholar, one can see how lesser mortals would still find it difficult to come to terms with the new philosophy throughout the succeeding century. It is for this reason that we need to survey the debate between revelation and reason which brings up the problem not only of miracle but also the interpretation of statements in Scripture that have been the cause of much religious dissension since the 16th century.

John Locke echoed what quite a number of the philosophers of the 17th century felt about the place of revelation in the Christian tradition when he wrote,

> 'Whatever God hath revealed, is certainly true; no doubt can be made of it. This is the proper object of faith: but whether it be a divine revelation, or no, reason must judge ... There can be no evidence, that any traditional revelation is of divine origin, in the words we receive it, and in the sense we understand it, so clear, and so certain, as that of the principles of reason ...'[43]

---

[42] Quoted in L. E. Elliott-Binns, *Religion in the Victorian Era*, Lutterworth Press, 1936[1966], page 170.

[43] John Locke, *An Essay Concerning Human Understanding*, Book IV, (continued...)

In other words, in the 17th-18th centuries it was politic to remain on the side of the church. The time had not come for a detailed criticism of the biblical records as indeed the revealed word of God. Spinoza was ahead of his time in maintaining that whatever is written down also reflects the opinions and judgements of the writers, so that the events related by them might be quite different from what was supposed to have happened. This is a very subtle, and perennial criticism of written records and we shall be returning to that theme later. But it was the idea of miracles that caused the most problems for the 18th century, and in particular for David Hume. He was not averse to making his controversial views known and published them in 1777. He wrote,

> '... [it appears, that] no testimony for any kind of miracle has ever amounted to a probability, much less to a proof; and that, even supposing it amounted to a proof, it would be opposed by another proof; derived from the very nature of the fact, which it would endeavour to establish. It is experience only, which gives authority to human testimony; and it is the same experience, which assures us of the laws of nature ... and therefore we may establish it as a maxim, that no human testimony can have such force as to prove a miracle, and make it a just foundation for any such system of religion.'[44]

A century before, instead of the miraculous, Spinoza defends what

---

[43](...continued)
Chapter xviii, § 10, edited by Roger Woolhouse, Penguin, 1997, page 613.

[44] David Hume, *An Enquiry Concerning Human Understanding*, (1777), in Oxford Philosophical Texts, *David Hume*, Oxford, 1999, Section X, Part II, pages 183-4.

is related in the Scriptures as due to natural causes, '... for whatsoever is contrary to nature is also contrary to reason, and whatsoever is contrary to reason is absurd, and, ipso facto, to be rejected.' [45]

While Old Testament criticism had begun in Germany in the early 19th century and was beginning to be known in England no one was prepared for the bomb shell of Charles Darwin's essay of the Origin of Species and Natural Selection which appeared in 1859. Not only did it seem that the creation narratives were simply mythical stories but the creation of humanity by God appeared to be undermined. But as Owen Chadwick has pointed out,

> 'The unsettlement of faith about the Bible in 1861-5 was directly caused by historians, or those who posed as historians in dealing with the texts of the Old and New Testaments. It was not caused by Darwin ... In one aspect the unsettlement was due not to the natural sciences but to the advance in study of ancient texts. In another aspect these students of ancient documents probably could not have written as they did unless they wrote in a climate of opinion formed by natural scientists and by philosophers. Geology disproved Genesis.' [46]

The late Victorian era in England was an unsettling time and it took at least half a century before religion and science came to some sort of understanding. On the Continent it was otherwise, as bishop Mandell Creighton observed in 1898,

---

[45] Spinoza, *A Theologico-Political Treatise*, Chapter vi, Transl. By R.H.M Elwes, Dover Publications, 2004, page 92.

[46] Owen Chadwick, *The Victorian Church, Part II*, Adam & Charles Black, 1972, page 3.

'When I have talked with men of science in other countries, I have found that it is impossible for a man who is a thinker to be in any sense whatever in friendship with the church; that this is not the case in this country makes me most hopeful for England and the mission which she has in the world.'[47]

The unsettlement in the Victorian period that Owen Chadwick remarked on included quite a lot of doubt about the life of Jesus. Some clergy doubted the miracles or the virgin birth and felt that they could not honestly recite the creeds in church. The liberal lives of Jesus that appeared at this time appealed to some who could not accept the face value of the miraculous in the gospels and Holman Hunt's pre-Raphaelite painting of Jesus, The Light of the World, expressed the feeling of many that religion would progress better without such doctrines as the virgin birth and the atonement. But the crisis of the early 20th century leading up to and including the Great War spelt the death of a 'liberal' Christian moralism without dogma. Instead, with the developing criticism of the New Testament, a neo-orthodoxy of the Bible began to make itself felt in the academic sphere, with Karl Barth (1886-1968) in particular who turned the debate back to the priority and reality of God. Barth emphasized the continuing revelation of God as absolute and the Scriptural texts as vehicles for that revelation. It was an all or nothing approach. God could not be approached from a human point of view as in the rationalist era that was now drawing to a close. (Adolph Harnack, who had been Barth's teacher, had argued for a dogma-free Christianity, based on our human desire for the truth and the historical and scientific examination of the records.) Emil Brunner (1889-1966), while differing from Barth in various

---

[47] Mrs Mandell Creighton, *Life and Letters of Mandell Creighton, Vol II*, Longmans Green, 1906, page 336.

ways also emphasized the radical nature of divine revelation,

> 'To believe in revelation is to believe in a miracle, in something that breaks into this world from beyond it ... The God of revelation is not the God of Deism ... He is the "Living God" who intervenes in natural happenings, who with His revelation bursts through the barriers of the natural possibilities of knowledge .. He is therefore, as Revealer and Redeemer, plainly the God of miracle; revelation too is plainly miraculous.'[48]

With these neo-orthodox affirmations we seem to have come full-circle back to the pre-17th century search for truth in the world as we know and experience it.

There was, however, a brief period just before and after the last war, when the historical investigation into the vocabulary of the Bible launched a new theory of how we come to an understanding of the meaning of Scripture as revelatory. It was assumed that particular words had a special meaning at the time they were used, both in the Old Testament writings and in the New Testament. This device assured the possibility of 'special' revelation about the acts of God and gave further evidence of traditional doctrines. One such was the understanding of anamnesis as reflecting in the first century CE, the idea that 'remembering' was not simply a mental act but a 're-enactment' or 'making effective', in the present of an event in the past. As applied to the Christian Eucharist this meant that older, pre-reformation doctrines of the real presence of Jesus could be re-habilitated. This biblical 'phase' has been superseded by the more rigorous, historical enquiry into the narratives of both the Old and New Testaments. But today the debate about miracle continues.

---

[48] Emil Brunner, *Revelation and Reason*, translated by Olive Wyon, SCM, 1947, page 294.

Tom Wright says,

> '... if we reject Hume's stance on miracles we are [not] bound to embrace a non-Humean world view in which a (normally absent?) God intervenes in the world in an apparently arbitrary and irrational fashion ... [as is] sometimes done by conservative apologists who are often interested [in] whether the Bible is believed to be 'true' or not ...'[49]

Wright is interested as perhaps seeing the miracles rather as the 'mighty works of God' - a long-awaited fulfilment of prophecy of the coming kingdom of God.

The critical examination of the biblical texts has brought into sharp relief the fact that all writing is influenced by the intentions, views and limitations of the author. This is seen clearly in the Hebrew bible where the early narratives were re-written by the 'chronicler(s)' to serve their particular slant on the people of God and his purposes. The New Testament gospels and other writings are, from the start, written from the Christian convictions that Jesus is Lord, the vindicated, crucified Messiah. On this account revelation is then a much less distinct, non unilateral affirmation that these writings contain a revelation of the divine. Spinoza and Hume are to that extent justified in their estimation of the value of Scriptural evidence that the texts should be estimated from within the body of Scripture and that for revelation, to be seen to be unique, there needs also an affirmation of its reasonableness. We shall be seeing that the all too human tendency to use scriptural texts as revealed truth in the interests of an orthodox view of worship has been a largely unthinking rejection of the right of reason to share in the valuation of worship as 'worship in spirit and in truth.'

---

[49] N.T. Wright, *Jesus and the Victory of God*, SPCK, 1996, pages 186 ff.

In the previous sections of this book I have attempted to show how the extraordinary energy of the 17th century philosophers set the agenda of the debate for the succeeding centuries in terms of how we understand both ourselves, God and the universe. In the ebb and flow of the arguments and against the background of immense social changes, the churches literally found it difficult to keep afloat. It seemed that all the accepted landmarks had been moved. The Roman Catholic church in Europe remained steadfastly against all notion of serious change in this eruption of 'modernity', other than to go forward, in the 19th century, into an even more radical conservative stance in the understanding of ecclesiastical authority and the validity of traditional doctrine. With the 39 Articles of Religion to maintain the status quo, the Church of England did not swerve after the Restoration and the Glorious Revolution of 1689, maintaining the 1662 Book of Common Prayer as the centre of its worship. While all the churches have renewed many aspects of their life of faith and worship there remains what some have seen as the baneful effects of the Enlightenment. Langdon Gilkey wrote as long ago as 1969,

> 'Any current theology ... that does not recognize and seek reflectively to deal with this presence of secularity, of doubt, of scepticism, and so of a sense of the meaninglessness of religious language inside the church as well as outside, and so inside the theologian and believer, is so far irrelevant to our present situation.'[50]

So now I turn to the very difficult question of how we may be able to understand God in terms which will resonate with a reasoned

---

[50] L .B. Gilkey, *Naming the Whirlwind: the renewal of God-language*, Indianapolis, Bobbs-Merrill, 1969, page 10.

estimation of faith in the context of the reality of life in the world today.

CHAPTER 4

God - Yesterday and Today

'There is but one living and true God, everlasting, without body, parts, or passions; of infinite power, wisdom, and goodness; the Maker, and Preserver of all things both visible and invisible.'

That quotation is part of Article 1 of the 39 Articles of the Church of England (1571), based on Thomas Cranmer's work. The other well known 'description' of God is that God is not only creator and eternal, but also omnipotent, omniscient, omnipresent and impassible. The language of both of these definitions is reflected in part in the 4th century Nicene creed, and in Christian hymns from the same period, as for example in the hymn attributed to St Ambrose (340-397):

'O strength and stay upholding all creation,
Who ever dost thyself unmoved abide.'

Part of our task will be to see whether the ideas of the Greek philosophers, that God is absolute, unchanging, infinite and eternal which Thomas Aquinas (1225-1274), most of all, brought into the discussion of the attributes of God, are compatible with those of the God of the believer who finds in worship one who responds in a personal love, compassion and understanding. But in fact the Old Testament narratives provided a basis for this 'identikit' of God which were taken on trust by both Jews and Christians until the 19th century rise of biblical criticism. So the figure of Yahweh guiding and judging Israel and the nations, passed into academic tradition as well as in the folk culture of the tribes and their relationship with the surrounding nations.[51] So if you take the revelation in Scripture to

---

[51] Cp Amos 3,2 'You only have I known of all the families of the earth; therefore I will punish you for all your iniquities.' Amos 9,1 'I saw the Lord standing beside the altar, and he said: Smite the capitals until the thresholds
(continued...)

be primary evidence, the early and mediaeval classical accounts of theism still obtain today, even though the Scriptural outlook is the actual basis for Christian faith. It is for that reason that when these traditions came under the scrutiny of 'reason' (as we have seen in particular with Spinoza's outright rejection of Scriptural traditions) many philosophers from the 18th century onwards were concerned to show that ideas such as omniscience and omnipotence could not be asserted of the actions of God without assuming a major contradiction of language in relation to life in our contemporary world. All the evidence of modern life is that we are autonomous beings and we even have to ask the question 'Who is God (if there is a god)?' Nevertheless, if there is a god, there is the need to make an attempt to 'describe' him and so classical theism is a reasonable place to begin in order that we may be able to modify it in ways that may make the idea of theism more acceptable from the viewpoint of the 21st century.[52]

---

[51](...continued)
shake, and shatter them on the heads of all the people; and what are left of them I will slay with the sword; not one of them shall flee away, not one of them shall escape.'

[52] The classical account of God has been modified in Charles Hartshorne's neo-classical account of God's existence as eternal but also influenced by events in the cosmos and in our lives. See *'Charles Hartshorne and the Existence of God* by D. W. Viney, State University Press of New York, Albany, 1985 for a lucid account of Hartshorne's bi-polar theory, especially pages 27-43.

God as Omnipotent

There is certainly a case to be made for God to be described as omnipotent if he is to be regarded as the creator of the universe and the sustainer of all that is. He is necessarily distinct from the whole of creation and from the point of view of comparison he is, as Anselm said, 'that than which a greater cannot be thought.'[53] Augustine in the Confessions made this point more poetically, and without controversy:

> 'But what is my God? I put my question to the earth. It answered, "I am not God", and all things on earth declared the same. I asked the sea and the chasms of the deep and the living things that creep in them, but they answered, "We are not your God. Seek what is above us." I spoke to the winds that blow, and the whole air and all that lives in it replied, "Anaximenes[54] is wrong. I am not God." I asked the sky, the sun, the moon and the stars, but they told me, "Neither are we the God whom you seek." I spoke to all things that are about me, all that can be admitted by the doors of the senses, and I said, "Since you are not my God, tell me about him. Tell me something of my God." Clear and loud they answered, "God is he who made us."'[55]

Creation, regarded today as the continually sustaining and cherishing of all the multifarious ways of biological mutations, is

---

[53] Anselm, *Proslogion*, c.5.

[54] Translator's footnote: Anaximenes of Miletus, the philosopher, who lived in the sixth century BCE. His teaching was that air is the first cause of all things.

[55] Augustine, *Confessions*, Book X, 6; transl. by R. S. Pine-Coffin, Penguin, 1961, page 212.

however, not the straightforward idea of modern 'creationists' that only God is the originator of ongoing creation. Nevertheless the boundless creative power to set and sustain the whole amazing process is beyond our imagining. But today the word 'omnipotent' (meaning that God can do anything) does imply a sort of continuing unilateral action on the part of the creator which is not true to the insights of modern thought. Much of the background 'evidence' for God as the almighty one came from the Old Testament stories. The 'exploits' of God in producing the plagues of Egypt by the hand of Moses in Egypt and the flight of the Israelites through the Red Sea, the punishments meted out among the rebellious people in their wilderness wanderings, the giving of the Law on Mount Sinai all reflect a deity who was awesome and to be greatly feared. As the writer of Hebrews says, 'It is a fearful thing to fall into the hands of the living God.' (Hebrews:10:31) This fear of a God of great authority and power is further advanced later on in Hebrews,

> 'For you have not come to what may be touched, a blazing fire, and darkness, and gloom, and a tempest, and the sound of a trumpet, and a voice whose words made the hearers entreat that no further messages be spoken to them. For they could not endure the order that was given, "If even a beast touches the mountain, it shall be stoned." Indeed, so terrifying was the sight that Moses said, "I tremble with fear." But you have come to Mount Zion and to the city of the living God, the heavenly Jerusalem, and to innumerable angels in festal gathering, and to the assembly of the first-born who are enrolled in heaven, and to a judge who is God of all ...'(Hebrews 12:18ff)

This typical manifestation of the 'holy' which is present in much of the Old Testament narratives and in other religions, was reinstated by Rudolph Otto (1869-1937) in his reaction to ideas of God as involved only in matters of morality, in his phrase, 'mysterium tremendum et fascinans'[56] - God is a holy, overwhelming, mysterious and fascinating power. But however much religious experience may be acceptable evidence to the reality of God the resulting echoes of the explosive power of deity is today queried by many who seek to understand what God is like in relation to our experience of life in modern times. It has often been maintained that to be God, he needs to be seen as quite other than the creation and so to be outside all the internal activity of the world and outside 'time'. This idea is perhaps more like the Greek Olympian gods of old who ruled from their rarified fastnesses in the mountain of Olympus,[57] and needs to be steadfastly rejected.

Is it possible then that the continual processes of creation and the sustaining of life in the world could point to the immanence of God, 'present' in the human and natural life of the world while yet remaining the origin of all that is? We shall see, in the next section on the 'personalness' of God, how necessary this idea is for a reasonable elucidation of God in our world. The biblical stories certainly express that understanding. This may be one way of softening, and making more realistic, the harsher idea of the god who, as powerful originator, sits back and looks on from outside. But there is the larger question as to whether God, as both transcendent and immanent, does intervene in affairs of humanity (as the biblical texts say he did). Let us look briefly at the 'problems' of an interventionist god.

Looking back over history, just in the Common Era, one sees

---

[56] Rudolph Otto, *The Idea of the Holy*, 1917, Pelican 1959, page 26ff.

[57] "No wind ever shakes the untroubled peace of Olympus; no rain ever falls there, or snow; but the cloudless firmament stretches around it on all sides and the white glory of sunshine is diffused upon its walls". (Homer)

most of all turmoil and war and mass slaughter even if there was a slow progress towards the stability of nations. Did God have any hand in this process? Or in more recent times the Holocaust and other human tragedies of dictatorships call into question the activity of a God who apparently was not able to stop nations and humanity continually falling into the abyss. Perhaps he was 'working' on the individual level and was able to bring some succour to the afflicted? But according to the psalmist's reproaches in the previous era it was always the bad who got off scot free and the good who suffered.

There is also the notorious issue of natural evil in the world. Evidently, as far as we know, God does not influence such things as the regular movements of tectonic plates in various places in the world or else (because he is true goodness) he would have possibly prevented the recent disastrous tsunami on December 26, 2004 that killed approximately 230,000 people. According to research these are regular features of the natural environment and, from a long way back, to the 16th century, there is evidence that there are naturally occurring movements beneath the oceans and land that can now be forecast - not to the day but at least to the coming half century. Or else, if there is a god of such goodness, could he not alter the rogue genes which cause so much cancer and disordered births of children? To ask these questions today is to expect the answer 'No', because medical research and geological discoveries tell us what is going wrong.

But how about the evidence of the miracles in the biblical narratives? It will be worthwhile to consider the miracles of Jesus, in three particular instances, as part of the problem of an interventionist god. Until the modern critical examination of the gospels in the 20th century, it was widely believed that the miracles in the gospels served to vindicate the divinity of Jesus. That is no longer the case for all who do not see the New Testament text as an infallible and divinely inspired account of the life of Jesus. Rather, the person of the historical Jesus has become much more genuine, and gained enormously in stature, through leaving to one side what was regarded, all through the mediaeval period, as God's interventions in the natural and human world seen in the miraculous events of the gospel stories. For many people today, including New Testament scholars, the miracles recounted by the evangelists are consonant with rather more normal explanations. For example the account in John 2:1-10, of the turning of the water into wine at Cana, which is the first of the 'signs' in the fourth gospel, can be shown to turn, not on the apparently enormous quantity of first class wine at the wedding feast, but on the crucial statement of the steward of the feast in John 2:10: '... you have kept the good wine until now' - which, in a comparable parable by Jesus in Mark 2:22, 'No one puts new wine into old wineskins; if he does the wine will burst the skins, and the wine is lost, and so are the skins; but new wine is for fresh skins', is a statement about the mission of Jesus to replace the old life of Israel with God's new creation. As Barnabas Lindars comments. '... though the narrative as history disappears [under form-critical analysis], an authentic tradition of Jesus comes to light.'[58] Secondly, the feeding of the multitude in John 6:1-15, suggests, says Lindars, while reflecting a real incident, 'that the actual event had a quasi-sacramental character: the meal was important for its meaning rather than for the physical nourishment of the people.'[59] Finally, this narrative is followed immediately by an account of Jesus walking on the sea, in John 6:16-21. The key to this incident lies probably in the fact that 'walking on the sea' can also be translated 'walking by the sea' and the significant climax of the story in Jesus' reply to the terrified apostles in verse 20, 'It is I;

---

[58] Barnabas Lindars, *The Gospel of John*, New Century Bible Commentary, Eerdmans Publ.Co., Grand Rapids, 1972, page 124.

[59] ibid. page 239.

do not be afraid.' is parallelled in Mark 6:50 in a slightly longer version and is a significant 'strengthening word' also to the early struggling Christian communities of Palestine.

It may be that these very short excerpts from the New Testament will do little to convince the reader that there is more to the miracle stories than meets the eye. But it has been worth while to make the point that divine incursions into creation and human life, as represented in the gospels, are not as simple as they appear to be in the sophisticated genre of 'gospel'. Moreover, Paul seems never to have been interested in the miraculous. The miracle stories of the gospels do not feature in his letters at all. One may have thought it would have been useful to confront the Gentiles with Jesus as a rather remarkable, contemporary wonder-worker. But for Paul, Jesus is 'the likeness of God', and, importantly for Paul, 'God was in Christ reconciling the world to himself, not counting their trespasses against them.'(2 Corinthians, 4:4b and 5:19) There is a sense in which we can say from the whole of the New Testament witness that Jesus, rather than being a wonder worker, became in himself the perfect man, the prototype of God's evolving new creation in humanity. While the miracles of the gospels always remain a challenge to any student of the New Testament, as for instance the raising of the son of the widow of Nain, (Luke 7:11-17), what is important above all for us is the New Testament's emphasis on the person of Jesus in relation to the 'character' of God which we have just been reviewing, and the resurrection of Jesus which we must now discuss.

The resurrection of Jesus, which no one witnessed, is in another category than 'miracle'. The validity of the whole gospel depends upon the received assertion of the early disciples that the resurrection and vindication of Jesus was the proclamation and actuality of the 'new creation' of God for all humanity. This view doesn't depend upon the story of the empty tomb but more upon the continuing activity of God in taking his part in the continuing creation. It is all the more remarkable for that!

The traditional understanding of the resurrection of Jesus and the consequent finding of the tomb being empty implies that God had, in some miraculous way, acted externally on the dead body of Jesus to raise him.[60] Was God working actively on the dead body of Jesus on the Saturday night before Easter Day? This would imply an interventionist god which I have in this section described as not in keeping with what we should wish to ascribe to the God whom Jesus called Father and who is for us the personal, loving and free God who is also transcendent, the creator of all that is. That the tomb was found empty is not the critical manifestation of what happened in the raising of Jesus - there could be many explanations for that. What is important is the fact of Jesus' resurrection which Paul states is a new creation in which we also will share,

> 'From now on, therefore, we regard no one from a human point of view; even though we once regarded Christ from a human point of view, we regard him thus no longer. Therefore, if any one is in Christ, he is a new creation; the old has passed away, behold, the new has come.' (2 Corinthians 5:16-17)

So if there has been any real intervention of God in the world it happened in the resurrection of Jesus by an act of new creation.[61]

---

[60] I owe this hypothetical idea of God's external action within the world, criticising the ideas of interventionist miracles, to an unpublished MPhil philosophy thesis of T. D. Pritchard, *God and the Concept of Miracle*, 2006.

[61] N. T. Wright's ascription of 'transformed physicality' to the risen Jesus may not be essentially different from what I have tentatively affirmed here but it is in the traditional mode of, and dependent upon, acceptance of the

(continued...)

This is embarrassing for our argument because while it seems the only explanation it is purely hypothetical and has to be taken on trust; as in fact does the first creation, also seen by no one! It seems that in creation and in the 'new creation' God has exhibited his immense powers and that in every other way he is not the god who will produce a rabbit out of the hat at our bidding. This says much for a more rational understanding of God than the theories of a god who, as we have seen in the pre-Enlightenment era, was claimed to be the cause of many natural processes

Perhaps we can then go on to put forward the view that he is a god who, in relation to the creation he has made, gives us and the dynamic energies of the natural world their autonomy within the ambit of his creative power? Then may we say that with all the potential power to hand, God is self-limited in relation to the whole creation?[62] Of course this could be construed to mean that God is only a little above, or on a par with, the powers of humankind and that, as Feuerbach (1804-1872) maintained,

> 'The divine being is nothing else than the human being, or rather, the human being purified, freed from the limits of the individual man, made objective- i.e., contemplated and revered as another, a distinct being.'[63]

---

[61](...continued)
empty tomb stories. See *The Resurrection of the Son of God*, SPCK, 2003 pages 476-479.

[62] See John Cottingham's persuasive arguments for God's relationship with an imperfect, material world in *The Spiritual Dimension*, Cambridge, 2005, Chapter 2: *Religion and science: theodicy in an imperfect universe*, pages 26-34.

[63] Ludwig Feuerbach, *The Essence of Christianity*, translated by George Eliot, Prometheus Books, New York, 1989, page 14.

But Feuerbach's problems are really much more a matter of language than of any sustained argument against there being a transcendent God who is both Creator and Father of humanity. This leads us to the 'other' side of God who has always, in the biblical records, been a 'conversant' God. How can he be 'in touch' with so many people, all the time and everywhere? We seem to have let ourselves in for an even more thorny problem!

God as Personal

It would follow, that if God is omnipotent, he is also omniscient, being aware of all happenings everywhere in the universe and in the world and so remembers all finite happenings in the past as well as in the present. In other words, God is always up-to-date on everything! While this essential knowledge of God must be considered a necessity if he is the creator and sustainer of all that is, there are here also other factors to be taken into account if such a God is not to be considered as having the 'evil eye'. For unless he is also personal, compassionate, loving, concerned with all that happens, he is none other than a despotic emperor playing an indescribably callous game with his creation as mere pawns. And there is more: unless God can be considered as susceptible to 'change' in relation to ourselves, and is also active within our experience of 'time' then he is still to be perceived as a deity who is impassively tucked away in some 'eternal' state of incomprehension of all that happens to us creatures, similar to Aristotle's Unmoved Mover. It would take another book to engage all these conceptions of what God 'must' be like,[64] so I shall be concentrating on the idea

---

[64] See the works of D. A. Pailin, *God and the Processes of Reality*, Routledge, 1989; *The Anthropological Character of Theology*, Cambridge, 1990; and
(continued...)

that God is 'personal' which will also bring to the discussion some of the other factors I have just mentioned.

A human person is, at least, a living, conscious creature, aware of others and able to respond to them, capable of compassionate understanding, holding in the memory thoughts and reflections, as well as being personally motivated in many kinds of ways. Memory is one of the essential bits of 'equipment' in human life. So God, in his relations with the creation must of necessity, if he is personal, qua God, have the ability to remember everything that was past and in the present, everywhere. There is a terminus ad quem to this feat however, as he cannot know what has not yet happened - he does not have foreknowledge of the future. Because God is often seen as 'non-human' he is often automatically thought to be beyond these finite, human traits. Leaving to one side at the moment what we briefly mentioned in the previous paragraphs that, according to Paul, Jesus is the likeness of God, and so God must at least have the extraordinary outgoing traits of Jesus, let us just concentrate on working through this apparent contradiction between the infinite, other and impassible understanding of God in classical theism and the possibility that God is actually 'personal', sympathetic, gracious and 'passible' in relation to us.

It is quite clear that, as I have already said, a God who is creator of all that is, and is of such a nature that he can sustain what he has begun in the universe, he must be at least as distinct from the nature of the continuing creation as we are from the rockets we fire into outer space. Yes, he is infinite, transcendent and necessarily without passions at the 'moment', and in the continuing process, of the creation. Yet even in that event he must also have had a vision of the beauty, the possibilities of creative replication in that extraordinary

---

[64](...continued)
Probing the Foundations, Pharos, 1994.

extension of the life of his own Being. The Genesis creation narratives (which in their origin sem to have had undertones both of priestly theologising and of 'native' explanations) capture for us something of the poetry and even music of what it might have been like to have been God in those first moments of determination. Such a God is not a wholly other, mechanistic designer. We might say that he deserves our worship in the sense that we are motivated to respond in wonder and joy. But is God capable of responding to us? There is a reasonable certainty that we can trust one who is intentionally and actively engaged in our sphere of life. If he is personal there is every chance that he wills what is good in all the changing circumstances of human life and the world. There have been many occasions throughout history when the records claimed that God had spoken to people, that they have understood the will of God for them and that life has changed as a result of the 'leading' of God. Pascal is one of them. From the conversation that the boy Samuel had with Yahweh (1 Samuel 3:1-18) to the meeting Paul had on the road to Damascus, one can point to a certain reality of communication. But in reality all is veiled between ourselves and the divine. In other words we have come to the point that we must admit that there is, in God, as far as we can give an account of his relationship with us, an element of mystery in his relation to the individual human being. Perhaps that is not a bad thing to say in our argument at this point for the mystery is not of the awesome and fascinating kind but the intimacy of mind (or self, or thought) with Mind. It has the recognizable lineaments of human friendship or meeting, without necessarily implying 'conversation'.

One factor in considering the encounter of humanity with God is the notion that God necessarily experiences 'change' in his personal connection with us and the world. It has been pointed out that unchangeableness in humans can signify atrophy and a withering away of life. This cannot be so of God who in his dynamic and living concern for all, wills to share in the changeableness of human life. The idea of the impassibility of God may seem to be all right if we are speaking about God in his Essence, but does it tally with what I have been saying in his awareness, and relationship with our life and predicament? It may seem that in proposing this we have strayed way beyond the normal understanding of what God should be like - aloof, silent and distant. In particular we might prefer to think of God as not being influenced by our notion of time and space. Our days and nights pass in continual succession, but it is often said that God is always experiencing the bliss of continual day and light. Much of these ideas of bliss as part of God's existence come from the neo-Platonists and the mystics. It may be true of course, but such ideas at once return us to the classical, theistic arguments for the impassibility of God and also influence our ideas of worship - of the God far 'above' us in the height of the heavens. (In fact 'time' is a relative concept and only serves to mark out the successive events as they happen. Isaac Newton[65] proposed that space and time were 'absolute', necessitated by God's existence; but this was criticised by Leibniz and others.)

In all that I have maintained that God is 'personal', as personal-as-can-be towards us, and is wholly immanent 'with us' we can acknowledge that in himself he is also the unchanging, infinite, perfect, Majestic Being who gives life to all and 'in whom we live and move and have our being.' This division of understanding between the transcendent and the personally immanent God is often a result of language - what we feel can and cannot be predicated of deity. So without prejudice it may be useful if we look at some of the divine-human encounters narrated in the Scriptural accounts and

---

[65] Isaac Newton, *Principia*, Scholium, in Philosophical Writings edited by Andrew Janiak, Cambridge, 2004, pages 64 ff.;and David A. Pailin, *Probing the Foundations*, Pharos, 1994, page 109.

to note the apparently artless language..

The Biblical 'experience' of God

The brilliant mathematician and scientist, Blaise Pascal, wrote in 'The Memorial', found sewn into his clothing at his death,
'The year of grace 1654 ...
'God of Abraham, God of Isaac, God of Jacob', not of philosophers and scholars.'[66]
Pascal had this personal revelation of God in the person of Jesus Christ on the night of 23rd November, 1654 which secured a permanent conversion and changed the course of his life.

The Hebrew writers of the stories in the Old Testament were nothing short of geniuses. Written from faith to faith their characterisations of the personal nature of the 'God of Abraham' cannot be surpassed. While the holy, awesome and transcendent God of the nation is often portrayed as acting with draconian powers, sweeping sinners off the face of the earth in judgement as in the frightening wilderness scene of Korah (Numbers 16:1-50), there always seems to be a sense of a relationship between God and the individual. Abraham, the pagan sojourner, and his wife Sarah, welcome the divine 'strangers' to a supper and is blessed by the Lord to become the father of many nations.(Genesis 18:1-9) Jacob, fleeing from the wrath of Laban his father in law, was blessed by God at the ford of Jabbok where his name was changed to Israel because, 'you have striven with God and with men, and have prevailed,' and Jacob concluded that, '... I have seen God face to face, and yet my life is preserved.'(Genesis 32:22-32) Moses 'meets' God in the incident of the burning bush and given his task to deliver

---

[66] Blaise Pascal, *Pensées*, Translated by A. J. Krailsheimer, Penguin, 1966, page 309.

Israel from their bondage in Egypt.(Exodus 3:1-6) In all these pre-historical, foundation myths of the chosen people the verisimilitude of the characterisation of a God who was in constant, 'human' touch is quite remarkable. In the more sophisticated narratives of the prophets, from Amos to the later Isaiah, the personal nature of the relationship between Yahweh and the individual is, if anything, stronger as the nation pursues its own decision to be ruled by kings and becomes a pawn in the hands of their enemies. The nation is personified in God's dealings with them and in Hosea the relationship is poignantly underlined, 'When Israel was a child, I loved him, and out of Egypt I called my son ... It was I who taught Ephraim to walk, I took them up in my arms; but they did not know that I healed them ... I led them with cords of compassion, with the bands of love.' (Hosea 11:1-4) Elsewhere the praise, laments and cries of the psalmists and the astonishing novella of Jonah and Job claim for the individual a special relationship with the divine. Then the experience of Jesus narrated in the gospels shew his faith in the God who is 'Father' and also the transcendent God who reveals himself in the event of the transfiguration of Jesus, 'This is my beloved son, listen to him' (Mark 9:7) and towards the end Jesus is represented as deep in prayer to God as he asks that the cup of suffering might pass from him.

While taking into account the fact that these personal religious experiences were written up, and so are coloured by the writers' own views, what divides us from them is that in the societies where religious experience appeared to be common, God was, without any doubt the foundation of all life and thought; (except for what the psalmist calls the fool: 'the fool says in his heart there is no God', Psalm 14:1). Today, in the West, there is no longer any great concern about God; indeed, if there is a god for us today, he is absent from our daily life. It has been said that this is the result of the Enlightenment. But more probably it is partly the result of ideas about the language of God being outmoded in terms of today's civilisation. The commonest ideas of what God is like are normally couched in the classical terms of an omnipotent and omniscient God, far removed from the concerns of society today. Those who seek to retain these concepts criticise the idea that God can, for instance, be both omnipotent and self-limited, or impassible and activated with loving concern. But without the personal relationship which I have outlined above, if God is thought of at all, he can only be considered an absentee landlord and we his unwilling, and perhaps rebellious, tenants. The biblical accounts of God might therefore be seen as ambivalent witnesses in providing a substantive rationality of a God who can be believed to be credible today. This is true not only of any logical apologetic but also in the details of Christian worship. It is to this latter that I turn now. But first of all it may be useful to summarize the 'possibilities' we have discovered about God in this recent discussion..

1. God is creator of all that is. He is transcendent and significantly separate from all that is made. He is unchangeable in majesty. But his activity in the continuing creation is, we assume, only one of interest, as the whole of the cosmos and the activities of humankind evolve. Therefore we may assume that he self-limits himself, having endued the processes with his energy.

2. In other ways God is not apart from the creation but has graceful sympathy with all that happens and with all that we do - which he remembers. This means that he is also 'changeable' through his sharing in our lives and in all that happens in nature. He is personal and that means his nature is one of love.

3. He is not a God who will interrupt the processes of life and nature either at his own whim or by our desire to have things

done for us which we might see as reasonable expressions of the divine within our lives. As such he is not an interventionist God but one who at all points shares our concerns for the future.

As a coda to this part of the book, archbishop William Temple, philosopher and theologian, in his book, Christus Veritas, has some cautionary and encouraging words which will link us to the specifically Christian concerns which follow:

' To say that we can understand this supreme Reality would be false; and if our view seemed utterly complete, that would condemn it. But we find what we have a right to hope for; we find that, though the supreme reality transcends our grasp, we are not ever merely baffled. As we move in thought from point to point, the mind is never checked by a sheer obstacle. In thinking of God as Christians have learnt to believe in him, the mind is always free; it is the finite before the Infinite, but its freedom proves its kinship. ... As we love him, we learn, for his sake and in his power, to love men. So loving, we become partakers of the divine nature, sharers in that divine activity whereby God is God.'[67]

---

[67] William Temple, *Christus Veritas*, Macmillan, 1930, [1924], pages 283-4.

CHAPTER 5

The New Testament Perspective

While I have so far looked at the possibilities of understanding God against the background of the new knowledge that came out of the Enlightenment and investigated what can be said of God in philosophical and logical terms, from now on I will take as axiomatic that the New Testament writers wrote from their deliberate conviction that the Jesus who was crucified and died had been raised to Lordship by God. But throughout the Middle Ages and the Reformation centuries, it was the death that Jesus died 'for us' which appeared to be the central understanding of Jesus, and in the late 19th century, liberal lives of Jesus were emphasizing his teaching and ministry. However, the New Testament authors, while not minimising these aspects of Jesus' life and death, are certain that the gospel preaching is of the raising of Jesus and so of the fulfilment of God's promises to Israel. In 1 Corinthians 15:3ff Paul is defending the resurrection of Jesus, and the resurrection of the dead at the close of the age, after what seems to be a traditional account being circulated about the life, death and resurrection of Jesus, and he writes, 'But in fact Christ has been raised from the dead, the first fruits of those who have fallen asleep...' And he writes in his introduction to the letter to the Romans, saying that he has been set apart for the gospel,

> 'the gospel concerning his Son, who was descended from David according to the flesh and designated Son of God in power according to the Spirit of holiness by his resurrection from the dead ...' (Romans 1:3-4)

In the Acts of the Apostles, Peter is said to have preached at the reception of Cornelius,

' you know ... how God anointed Jesus of Nazareth with the Holy Spirit and with power ... And we are witnesses to all that he did both in the country of the Jews and in Jerusalem. They put him to death by hanging him on a tree; but God raised him from the dead on the third day and made him manifest ... to us who were chosen as witnesses ...' (Acts 10:34-43)

It seems that the disciples' conviction that Jesus was vindicated, raised by God, changed their whole outlook on their Jewish monotheistic faith. A man had, seemingly, been put on an equal footing with God - or at least shared in the dominion of God. They knew who he was, having sat at table with him. So was he 'just' a man, if a very remarkable one? From the time of Nicea in 325, for the next century and a quarter, the debate over the personal nature of Jesus went on. Finally the fifth century pope Leo the Great (died in 461) summarized a definition of the relationship between God and Jesus - it was just a 'description' and not an explanation - which has remained the accepted traditional account of the matter. (Creeds and statements of belief were intended to exclude what were regarded at any time as 'heretical' views of the nature of Jesus and his relation to God rather than explanations.) It is useful for us to discuss this problem - gently, as much ink has been spilt and many lesser tomes have been produced - as I shall need to refer to the lordship of Jesus in the following liturgical discussions.

Leo's Tome stated:

'... Thus there was born true God in the entire and perfect nature of true man, complete in his own properties, complete in ours. ... The Son of God therefore came down from his throne in heaven without withdrawing from the Father's glory, and entered this lower world, born after a new order, by a new mode of birth

> ... From his mother the Lord took nature, not sin. Jesus Christ was born from a virgin's womb, by a miraculous birth: and yet his nature is not on that account unlike to ours, for he that is true God is also true man.'[68]

This was affirmed at the council of Chalcedon in 451. The creed of Nicea (325) had already affirmed that Jesus Christ was,

> 'the only-begotten Son of God, begotten of his Father before all worlds, God of God, Light of Light, very God of very God, begotten, not made, being of one substance with the Father.'

and this is still used in our worship today.

While Matthew and Luke write about the miraculous birth of Jesus, in John's gospel the birth is said to be through the heavenly Logos who becomes flesh, the flesh of the humanity of Jesus. And Paul refers to the birth of Jesus in Galatians 4:4-5,

> 'When the time was fully come God sent forth his Son, born of woman, born under the law, to redeem those who were under the law, so that we might receive adoption as sons.

Whatever the truth that lies behind these stories of a remarkable birth, and in Luke of the infancy narratives, the humanity of Jesus, as recorded in the synoptic gospels, is of a genuinely human personality. Hindsight after the resurrection event might have caused the elaboration of the birth stories but it is the other way round as far as the living Jesus is concerned - he is truly human - and raises the question for us, 'How then can he also be God's Son? - to

---

[68] Leo the Great, in *The Later Christian Fathers*, translated and edited by Henry Bettenson, Oxford, 1970, pages 279-280.

the extent that John's gospel can have Jesus say, 'I and the Father are one.' But we have to note that the New Testament writers do not actually call Jesus 'God'. The Prologue to St John's gospel speaks of the Logos assuming human flesh but does not actually say that the 'resultant' human was God. It is often assumed that Jesus was God 'enfleshed' but Paul appears always to speak of the revelation of God in and through the Lord whom he 'met' on the Damascus road.

Many of the early and late mediaeval pictures of Jesus is of the 'God-Man' striding the earth. This confusion of the 'natures', as the patristic authors would say, and as the so called Athanasian creed asserts, 'neither confounding the Persons, nor dividing the Substance', is an easily understandable mistake but it doesn't answer our question. In an important essay,[69] Professor Morna Hooker points out that while the Chalcedon definition was probably inevitable, excluding what was perceived at the time to be heretical ideas, the New Testament never speaks of Jesus as God nor actually describes 'how God became man'. This despite the opening verse in John, that 'the word was God' which she says has to be understood in the context of the whole gospel. John, being written probably at the end of the first century, was reflecting the local controversies between the Christian and Jewish communities. The metaphysical language of Chalcedon has, since the 5th century, been read back into the New Testament without warrant and left us with that problem! (We shall be seeing later how the doctrine of the atonement has also been read back into the New Testament.) As Professor Hooker says,

' ... the Chalcedonian definition is not a direct 'translation' of what is being said in the New Testament into another set of

---

[69] Morna D. Hooker, *Chalcedon and the New Testament*, in The Making and Remaking of Christian Doctrine, ed. by Sarah Coakley and David A. Pailin, Oxford, 1993, pages 73-91.

terms, for the questions its authors addressed were totally different from those which exercised the authors of the New Testament. When it comes to interpreting what the latter were trying to say, we must always remember to take off spectacles which have in any way been tinted with Chalcedonian beliefs ... the first Christians ... were aware only that in Jesus of Nazareth God had spoke to them in a way which led them ever more confidently to identify the revealer with the revealed.'[70]

To cope with the perceived problems bequeathed to us by the Chalcedonian definitions, at the turn of the 20th century the idea of a *kenosis*, a self-emptying of God so that as man he had none of the divine prerogatives of God, was taken up as a solution of how God can become man. But the idea of the universe existing, as it were, on a pre-programmed set of orbits, while Jesus lived out his 30 or so odd years before the final denouement, seemed to many to be distinctly odd! Archbishop William Temple in 1934 demolished that idea in his book, *Christus Veritas*,[71] and suggested, as an alternative, in a detailed and lively argument, that Jesus became not only a man, but Man.

'He more than others is humanity focussed in one centre. [Mankind or Humanity is a close-knit system of mutually

---

[70] ibid. pages 90-91.

[71] 'He who is always God became also Man - not ceasing to be God the while. For the Incarnation was effected "not by conversion of the Godhead into flesh, but by taking of Manhood into God"'; and, 'To say that God the Eternal Son at a moment of time divested himself of omniscience and omnipotence in order to live a human life, seems to me just the kind of thing that no event occurring on this planet could justify.' William Temple, *Christus Veritas*, MacMillan & Co, 1930 [1924], pages 140-141.

influencing units] ...Into this system of mutually influencing units Christ has come, but here is a unit perfectly capable, as others are only imperfectly capable, both of personal union with all other persons and of refusing to be influenced by the evil of his environment. It is this more than anything else which proves him to be more and other than his fellow-men ... Thus in a real sense Christ is not only a man; he is Man.'[72]

The sense here is that God, who is immanent as well as transcendent, as we have already discussed, does not cease to be God in the incarnation of the Son as Jesus Christ. It is not a trick of divinity but presumably an 'expression' of the divine love. However, as William Temple, in a typical observation, says,

'Our effort, therefore, to deal with the problems of belief in the Incarnation must start with the confession, or rather with the claim, that from the nature of the case their solution cannot be found by us. If any man says that he understands the relation of deity to humanity in Christ, he only makes it clear that he does not understand at all what is meant by an Incarnation.'[73]

Today, however, it is extremely difficult, three quarters of a century after Temple was writing, to begin to understand 'Incarnation', so great has been the increase of scientific knowledge and theory, and the degree of scepticism by the early 21st century. However, it is important for us to make the effort to consider, if not to understand, the personality of Jesus in relation to God as this has been handed down to us in the accounts. Then the conviction that he is indeed the risen Lord, as those accounts testify, has some greater content.

---

[72] ibid. pages 151-153.

[73] ibid. page 139.

Presumably the disciples went through that same process living with Jesus, as we are doing in trying to come to some understanding of the claim that he was divine, noticing the mystery of his personality which could often strike them with, at times, a sense of enormous astonishment and at other times of fear. It is the extraordinary event of the transfiguration, at a watershed in the ministry of Jesus, which reflects both their inability to understand what is 'going on' and also our difficulties in coming to terms with this divine/human personality whom we acknowledge as Lord. But this extraordinary event has also within it the possibility of unlocking the mystery of his person. Whether the transfiguration account belongs to personal testimony of the three disciples who witnessed it, or not, in reading the narrative of the synoptic gospels one cannot but be struck by the apt allusions to the Old Testament - the Shekinah of God, the voice from the cloud, the vision of Moses and Elijah, and in Luke the whole idea of the 'exodus' of Jesus. Jesus is intended to be seen as the fulfiller of Israel's hope. It has also been suggested that the whole episode reflects the inner mind of Christ, for as archbishop Michael Ramsey pointed out in his study of the transfiguration, 'The Transfiguration does indicate that the messianic age is already being realized: Jesus is the Messiah, the kingdom of God is here, the age to come is breaking into this world.'[74] In many respects the narrative is a theological portrait of Jesus. In terms of understanding the personality of Jesus in relation to the Father the transfiguration seems to be presented by the gospel authors as a major clue to that relationship in whatever way we may be led to understand it. So Ramsey concludes his study in the terms of the gospel,

---

[74] A.M. Ramsey, *The Glory of God & the Transfiguration of Christ*, Longmans, Green & Co, 1949, page 119.

'He who is transfigured is the Son of Man; and, as he discloses on Mount Hermon another world, he reveals that no part of created things and no moment of created time lies outside the power of the Spirit, who is Lord, to change from glory into glory.'[75]

It is interesting that Professor C. F. D. Moule arrived at a very similar theory of the relation of the risen Lord to the Church and to humankind, as archbishop Temple did for the relationship of the human life of Jesus to God. Moule proposed that,

' ... to his followers Jesus showed himself alive - totally alive with transcendent life, the life of the age to come - confirming his identification with that divinely powerful presence that had been seen in his ministry, but now without the limitations of time and place. To any of them anywhere he came known to be present with a divine, inclusive presence ... Christians are parts and organs of a living organism, which is Christ himself (1 Corinthians 12:13): his vital force is theirs.'[76]

From the Pauline letters Christ is often spoken of in a way that seems to indicate that he is the ambience in which the Christian lives. To be 'in Christ' is to share that new life of the second Adam in whom there has been a new creation effected through the vindication of Jesus by God.

'For Paul, Jesus Christ, though still a vividly individual person, "who loved me and gave himself for me"' (Galatians 2:20), is at

---

[75] ibid. page 147.

[76] C. F. D. Moule, Jesus of Nazareth and the Church's Lord, in *Forgiveness and Reconciliation*, SPCK, 1998, pages 85-86.

the same time larger than the individual. He is the very ambience in which Christian life is lived.'[77]

But Professor Moule also shows, perhaps in an even greater degree than archbishop Temple, a sense of humility before the mystery, writing, 'No doubt these speculations are rash and crudely framed. They illustrate some of the difficulties that arise if one is dissatisfied with rationalizing expedients.'[78] Moule opened his essay by citing some of these 'expedients' such as substituting the 'Spirit of God', or stressing the identity between Jesus of Nazareth and the Church, for what the New Testament writers say was their experience of the actual presence of the risen Lord to them.

Our own identification of Jesus as the risen Lord can only gain in clarity from a continuing personal appraisal of the New Testament and our own experience of a reasoned belief in God who Jesus called 'Father'.

---

[77] ibid. page 86.

[78] ibid. page 92.

CHAPTER 6

The Liturgical Movement

We discussed earlier how the Tractarian revival sought to bring to the forefront of the Church of England a revived understanding of the church as a divinely ordered society in which the Eucharist would be restored to a central position in worship. The later 19th century witnessed strong support for this and indeed for a greater use of that kind of ceremonial which was believed to be allowed by the rubrics, such as lighted candles on the altar, a surpliced choir and the wearing of vestments. While certain priests in the church adopted roman usages - and were to that extent eccentric in relation to the majority of parishes - by and large the beautifying of services continued to be accepted in many parishes over the next half century. But 'decorum' in worship was not the only concern.

There was a real desire of many in the church to update the prayer book to be more suitable both for the modern world and to allow new insights about worship. For many people, especially the clergy, the 1662 Prayer Book was limited by its reflection of the theological controversies of the Reformation as well as by its Tudor language. As the outcome of the 1903 decision that the prayer book was too narrow for modern needs, eventually the 1928 Prayer Book was offered to parliament but was turned down. It was out of this debacle that there arose in the church the grassroots movement that secured what came to be known as the Parish and People movement to encourage parishes to turn from having a Mattins main service on Sunday morning to a Parish Communion eucharist. There was also to be more participation in the services for the laity. In the very different milieu of the Roman Catholic church on the Continent a parallel movement had already begun in France and Germany, giving support and inspiration to those who were hoping for a renewal of worship here. These pastoral initiatives then sparked off a more academic movement for the examination of the various rites of worship in comparison with what was becoming known from the earlier centuries, in particular of the fourth century.

The academic study of liturgy may be said to have begun with the Maurist Benedictine monks of St-Germaine-des Prés who, from 1672 onwards began the process of identifying manuscripts, liturgical as well as literary, making it possible to sort out the genuine from the rest.

> 'The Maurist school of scholarship proved a turning point in the inauguration of modern philological and historical method by attempting to achieve a complete accounting of all the material available.'[79]

Manuscript evidence for liturgical services is very thin on the ground and the earliest manuscript is not earlier than the 8th century, while scattered remnants are to be found in the writings of bishops, such as those of Cyril of Jerusalem and literary compositions purporting to be genuine 'apostolic' literature such as the Apostolic Constitutions of the 4th century.[80] But as Bradshaw points out[81] it is not easy to decide whether any liturgical description in the accounts that have come down to us represents what was actually the practice of a church or region. For this we need something more than the philological method of literary discrimination and comparison pioneered by the Maurist monks.

Texts are only one aspect of Christian worship traditions. There

---

[79] John Fenwick & Bryan Spinks, *Worship in Transition*, T&TClark, 1995, page 14.

[80] See Paul F. Bradshaw, *The Search for the Origins of Christian Worship*, SPCK, 2002, pages 74 ff.

[81] ibid. pages 14ff.

is the need also to ask what was the background of their provenance and, as far as we can, seek to set the evidence against the theological concerns of the time. It had been assumed by many in the past that the patterns of worship arose from a single source in the early years of the first century which only later became diversified in the East and West. This also led several to assume that early liturgical texts were a mirror of the orthodoxy which some scholars would like to see vindicated, and to create a link to the apostolic age and even to Jesus. In fact, as several scholars have expressed recently,[82] the opposite seems to have been the case and that there was great diversity to begin with in the first three centuries in worship and that unification came in the late fourth century. Despite the renewal of the service books in all the churches in the past 30 years, there is still a lot to be done to elucidate the origins, growth and meaning of Christian worship. The same is true of Jewish worship which, for a long time, was also considered to have been 'fixed' in the early first century CE.

While the historical origins of worship are important to understand today, it has now also become urgent that we see Christian worship in our own context. It is interesting that not a few of our Christian contemporaries today seem to find the Enlightenment not as a breath of new life and understanding but rather as a threat to their traditional faith and practice. On the contrary, faith in the risen Lord and belief in the God whom he called 'Father' can only be 'ratified' for us today when we are able to use those insights of human knowledge that sprang from the new philosophy and natural sciences as well as the historical and revelatory bases of Christian faith.

However, I am not concerned so much in the broad sweep of

---

[82] See Paul F. Bradshaw, *The Search for the Origins of Christian Worship*, SPCK, 2002, page 8.

liturgy as it is being scrutinised today, but in particular assertions of a theological nature such as references to the death of Jesus, or to more recent theories of consecration in the eucharist and of remembrance and presence. So it is to consideration of these that I now turn, prefaced by the following 'caveat'.

A caveat

It has sometimes been the case that in discussion of liturgical usages, any change towards greater simplicity, and related to more theological concerns rather than with the perceived essentials of tradition, has aroused the criticism that it is a move towards a less 'catholic' or a more 'evangelical' understanding of what should happen in worship, (or vice-versa). Also the deep divisions since 1689 between Anglicans and the Free Churches have remained in the corporate consciousness so that any movement away from catholic Anglicanism or evangelical Anglicanism towards the Free church tradition has also been deeply distrusted. This is still true today even when there has been a certain consensus between the churches over the reforms of worship. So if in the following discussions there appears to be a move towards a less traditional outlook in any given sphere of liturgy, that does not mean that I am appealing to some part of the Church of England or to Non-Conformity in the conclusions I reach. I hope to remain neutral in academic discussion as far as ecclesiastical traditions are concerned, seeking only to look at any particular issue in terms of how we understand it both in relation to God and also in the light of the search for truth in the reality of today's world, as we have discussed those issues earlier.

CHAPTER 7

Atonement and the Eucharist

There are several 'short cuts' to an understanding of why Christ died. These depend upon taking the words about sacrifice and redemption and all the ancillary words relating to the cross and the death out of their context in the New Testament and then to treat them literally. This is also a hazardous way of treating what Paul has written, for as E. P. Sanders has shown, Paul is not consistent in his thoughts. His letters reveal this. He is always having to respond to particular crises among the young communities and his arguments have to be understood in the particular context in which he was involved. For example, he is wrestling with his Jewish sensibilities - that the Law is good and yet in Jesus the law has been abrogated, at least for the Gentiles.[83] Paul is so often treated as having a systematic theology but this can only be achieved if we make a harmonization of his thought which he never accomplished. To a large extent this was the procedure adopted over the last 1600 years by eminent scholars and churchmen. So in regard to terms used for explaining why Christ died, there has been no consensus, but terms like - substitution, propitiation or expiation - have gained a certain acceptance and have been woven into liturgical thought and practice over the centuries. We shall opt for the longer route, beginning with the life of Jesus and seeing in the gospel portrayal of his quite short mission, and perhaps in his own understanding of the 'aim' of his life, the factors which led to his execution in Jerusalem.

---

[83] 'Paul appeals to Abraham to argue against the requirement of circumcision, although one of the main points of the Abraham stories in Genesis is that Abraham and his descendants must be circumcised; those who are not circumcised will be 'cut off'.' (Genesis 17:9-14) E. P. Sanders, *Paul*, in Early Christian Thought in its Jewish Context, eds. John Barclay and John Sweet, Cambridge, 1996, pages 117ff.

St Mark

> 'Now after John was arrested, Jesus came into Galilee, preaching the gospel of God, and saying, "The time is fulfilled, and the kingdom of God is at hand; repent, and believe in the gospel."' (Mark 1:14-15)

This good news of God, which, as we have seen, was central to Paul's preaching, was about the new life shared by Jesus with any who came to him seeking help and mercy - willing to be turned round in their life through repentance. The typical aspect of this lay in the healing of many people as Jesus went about the villages and towns of Galilee and Judea. But in this initial announcement there is the larger challenge that the time for all this was quite short, for God's sovereign rule, here in Palestine, was just round the corner, so to speak. There was no time to lose. Jesus was the herald of the rule of Israel's God.

If Mark's gospel is read straight through, the urgency of Jesus' message and concern appear quite clearly. Whatever the editorial recasting of the life of Jesus by Mark, a certain 'plan' emerges with the calling of disciples, the itinerant preaching, healing and care for all whom he met. Inevitably, as on the Sabbath when he healed the man with a withered hand, there was opposition -

> 'The Pharisees went out, and immediately held counsel with the Herodians against him, how to destroy him.' (Mark 3:6)

But despite claims that he was possessed by Beelzebul and that he cast out demons by the prince of demons, Jesus' ministry was effective everywhere, except perhaps in his own city of Nazareth where he taught in the synagogue,

> '... and many who heard him were astonished, saying, "Where did this man get all this? What is the wisdom given to him? What

mighty works are wrought by his hands! Is not this the carpenter, the son of Mary and brother of James and Joses and Judas and Simon, and are not his sisters here with us?" And they took offense at him.' (Mark 6:2-3)

The records of his teaching by pithy parables seem to have occasioned a large response. The parables of the kingdom highlight Jesus' own concern that in everyday circumstances the kingdom of God was appearing.

> "The kingdom of God is as if a man should scatter seed upon the ground, and should sleep and rise night and day, and the seed should sprout and grow, he knows not how. The earth produces of itself, first the blade, then the ear, then the full grain in the ear. But when the grain is ripe, at once he puts in the sickle, because the harvest has come." (Mark 4:26-28)

Famously, Jesus also directs a parable against the religious establishment towards the end of the ministry in the story of the Vineyard, which concludes with the denouement,

> '... the tenants said to one another, 'This is the heir; come, let us kill him, and the inheritance will be ours. And they took him and killed him, and cast him out of the vineyard. What will the owner of the vineyard do? He will come and destroy the tenants, and give the vineyard to others. Have you not read this scripture: 'The very stone which the builders rejected has become the head of the corner; this was the Lord's doing, and it is marvellous in our eyes'?"
> And they tried to arrest him ... (Mark 12:7-12)

It is in the meals Jesus had with the disciples and with any who cared to share with them, that the uniqueness of Jesus' own drawing power is most manifest. So, after the call of Levi, Mark notices that,

> '... as he sat at table in his house, many tax collectors and sinners were sitting with Jesus and his disciples.' (Mark 2:15)

and in Bethany, towards the end,

> '... in the house of Simon the leper, as he sat at table, a woman came with an alabaster flask of ointment of pure nard, very costly, and she broke the flask and poured it over his head',

Jesus replies to a comment that the use of such precious spikenard was a waste,

> "She has done what she could; she has anointed my body beforehand for burying. And truly, I say to you, wherever the gospel is preached in the whole world, what she has done will be told in memory of her." (Mark 15:3 & 8-9).

But it is the last meal that Jesus had with the disciples which has rightly come in for the most comment. The accounts of the Last Supper in the Synoptic gospels and Paul, while diverse, give the impression that Jesus foresaw that his life was in imminent danger,

> 'And as they were eating, he took bread, and blessed, and broke it, and gave it to them, and said, "Take; this is my body." And he took a cup, and when he had given thanks he gave it to them, and they all drank of it. And he said to them, "This is my blood of the covenant, which is poured out for many. Truly, I say to you, I shall not drink again of the fruit of the vine until that day when I drink it new in the kingdom of God."' (Mark 14:22-25)

There were intimations in the gospel that Jesus had foretold that he would be put to death . Three times, it is said, Jesus told the disciples about this. On the last occasion, Mark records it,

> 'And they were on the road, going up to Jerusalem, and Jesus was walking ahead of them; and they were amazed, and those who followed were afraid. And taking the twelve again, he began to tell them what was to happen to him, saying, "Behold, we are going up to Jerusalem; and the Son of man will be delivered to the chief priests and the scribes, and they will condemn him to death, and deliver him to the Gentiles; and they will mock him, and spit upon him, and scourge him, and kill him; and after three days he will rise." (Mark 10:32-34)

Whether or not these three warnings by Jesus can be attributed to him or to others after the event does not matter a great deal. For in the temple Jesus deliberately, it seems, challenged the temple authorities,

> 'And he entered the temple and began to drive out those who sold and those who bought in the temple, and he overturned the tables of the money-changers and the seats of those who sold pigeons; and he would not allow any one to carry anything through the temple. And he taught, and said to them, "Is it not written, 'My house shall be called a house of prayer for all the nations'? But you have made it a den of robbers." (Mark 11:15-17)

In a sense the die was cast and Jesus would inevitably, short of a 'miracle', fall into the hands of his enemies, the chief priests of the day. In the events following on the Last Supper, in the garden in Gethsemane, Jesus is said to have prayed alone to God,

'... that, if it were possible, the hour might pass from him. And he said, "Abba, Father, all things are possible to you; remove this cup from me; yet not what I will, but what you will."' (Mark 14:35-36)

As it turned out we see the mission for the proclamation of the coming kingdom of God terminated in the crucifixion of the Son of man, as he called himself. The raising of Jesus 'after three days', is not actually reported by Mark, but the women at the tomb are told,

"Do not be amazed; you seek Jesus of Nazareth, who was crucified. He has risen, he is not here; see the place where they laid him. But go, tell his disciples and Peter that he is going before you to Galilee; there you will see him, as he told you." (Mark 16:6-7).

In these brief extracts from the gospel of Mark we see a man whose whole life is concerned with sharing his gifts of teaching, healing, friendship and, not least, leadership with all whom he came across. Did he have an aim in all this? There is a verse in Mark which some say pinpoints that,

"... whoever would be great among you must be your servant, and whoever would be first among you must be slave of all. For the Son of man also came not to be served but to serve, and to give his life as a ransom for many." (Mark 10:44-45)

What did Jesus mean by 'ransom' and to whom should it be paid? Those questions tantalised theologians from at least the 4th century CE and strange theories were devised to explain the death of Jesus. They are not our concern at the moment. A more recent comment has been put forward by bishop Tom Wright in his book, *Jesus and*

The Victory of God. After a prolonged discussion throughout the book of Jesus' mission, he declares at the end of the book,

> 'I propose, as a matter of history, that Jesus of Nazareth was conscious of a vocation: a vocation, given him by the one he knew as 'father', to enact in himself what, in Israel's scriptures, God had promised to accomplish all by himself. He would be the pillar of cloud and fire for the people of the new exodus. He would embody in himself the returning and redeeming action of the covenant God.'[84]

However, it remains to be proved that Israel saw itself still in 'exile' at the time of Jesus and that the young prophet from Nazareth was the self proclaimed redeemer of his people. There have been few positive evaluations of Jesus' intentions, and Tom Wright's essay is at least a relief from the continual repetition that Jesus died for our sins. As we have seen, apart from this single verse in Mark about a 'ransom', there is little that can be said of Jesus in the gospel that he died to save us from our sins. There is the call to repent - that is, to turn around, away from a sinful life, to enter into a life which Jesus already in his life time is sharing with those who respond to his call as a foretaste of that kingdom of God which was already at hand. So we must turn now to Paul who is often reputed to have a certainty that what happened on Calvary, in tragic and bloody circumstances, was the forgiveness of humanity's sins. Let us find out.

St Paul

In about 54-55 CE Paul was writing to the church at Corinth, that is about 20 years after the crucifixion. He states as a matter of fact,

---

[84] N. T. Wright, *Jesus and the Victory of God*, SPCK, 1996, page 653.

'For I delivered to you as of first importance what I also received, that Christ died for our sins[85] in accordance with the scriptures. (1 Corinthians 15:3)

Then Paul goes on to state that the risen Lord has been seen by many and finally by himself. In other words, Paul's understanding of what happened in Christ's death on the cross was that the dominion of evil has been broken, once for all, because Christ has been raised. The death of Jesus was certainly the freeing of us from the power of sin - sin had been 'expiated', to use a Jewish term - but that event had no reference to God for God himself was in Christ, as Paul later says,

> 'in Christ God was reconciling the world to himself, not counting their trespasses against them.'(2 Corinthians 5:19)

God is the initiator of our remaking and has shared the suffering both of our sinful condition and of the death of Christ. We might venture a point of view here and say if there was a sacrifice, God was the subject and not the object of it.

It has been noted that in Paul's letters there is very little said about repentance and forgiveness. Rather he is concerned that as Christians, (and he is writing to Christians), we must believe in the gospel. For in Christ we have changed our allegiance from the dominion of sin and evil to the lordship of the risen Lord. This is put strongly in the introduction to the previous quotation from 2 Corinthians,

---

[85] It has been suggested that 'for our sins' was an addition by Paul. For instance Acts does not connect the death of Christ specifically with forgiveness. But Dr Morna Hooker discounts that. See M. D. Hooker, *Not ashamed of the Gospel*, Paternoster Press, 1994, page 21.

'For the love of Christ controls us, because we are convinced that one has died for all; therefore all have died. And he died for all, that those who live might live no longer for themselves but for him who for their sake died and was raised. From now on, therefore, we regard no one from a human point of view; even though we once regarded Christ from a human point of view, we regard him thus no longer. Therefore, if any one is in Christ, he is a new creation; the old has passed away, behold, the new has come.'

He wrote to the Galatians earlier in the same vein, saying,

'Grace to you and peace from God the Father and our Lord Jesus Christ, who gave himself for our sins to deliver us from the present evil age, according to the will of our God and Father; to whom be the glory for ever and ever.' (Galatians 1:4-5)

Nothing could be clearer than this statement that what 'happened' in the crucifixion was God's initiative in breaching the gap between humanity and himself, so bringing about the new creation in the raising of Christ and the new and final age of the creation. So, while Paul reiterates the tradition that Jesus died for our sins, the underlying truth was much wider, embracing humanity's actual existence and relationship with God and with one another. In Christ there was to be formed a new creation, a new life for the final age of the kingdom of God.[86]

The death of Jesus was in the first instance a result of the

---

[86] Dr Morna Hooker points out that, 'We are so accustomed to thinking of the death of Christ as itself the saving act of God that we perhaps forget that for the early Christians their first awareness that God was at work in these events came with the resurrection. ibid. page 17.

antagonism on the part of the Jewish hierarchy. For, as Mark notices in 15:10, Pilate recognized that it was out of envy that they had delivered Jesus up for punishment. Paul and the other writers in the New Testament frequently use terms such as sacrifice, redemption, expiation, the blood of Christ, 'paschal lamb', in connection with Jesus' death. But whatever the terms used, from the law courts or of forensic judgement or the Torah, Paul is always bringing into focus the figure of Jesus as the one who not only brought about the redemption of the race but also the renewal of the whole cosmos, and whatever traditional terms are applied to the death they are always metaphorical. For Paul, Jesus is the last Adam, (1 Corinthians 15:47) and has become for us 'a life-giving spirit.' We cannot read back into the New Testament later ideas of 'atonement', still less can the sufferings of Jesus be made into an act of reconciliation - as Kenneth Grayston has noted, '... Nowhere is it said that faithful, devout Jews bear witness to God and his commandments by suffering, or even dying.'[87] This faith of the early Christians that what Jesus had done, as they said 'once for all'-*'apax* - depended upon their acceptance that Jesus had been vindicated by God in the resurrection. The risen Lord was the 'guarantee' that in and through his death humanity has been brought to this amazing possibility of a new start, a new creation with Christ. As we shall be seeing later, Paul writes of the death, at the end of his account of the Institution narrative of the Last Supper, ' ... as often as you eat this bread and drink the cup, you proclaim the Lord's death until he comes.' (1 Corinthians 11:26), that it is an eschatological event, i.e. not the historical, once-for-all crucifixion that should be proclaimed, but the 'threshold' as it were, which has enabled us to cross from

---

[87] See Kenneth Grayston's essay, *Atonement and martyrdom*, in *Early Christian Thought in its Jewish Context*, ed. by John Barclay & John Sweet, Cambridge, 1996, pages 250-263.

death to life. One important observation by E. P. Sanders is that Paul, despite the first five chapters of Romans beginning with 'sin', actually begins in his thought and theology, not with 'sins' but with the saving facts of Christ's death and resurrection. In other words the 'solution', in Paul's thought, precedes the 'plight' of humanity, and salvation is from the old aeon to the lordship of Christ,

> ' ... the prime significance which the death of Christ has for Paul is not that it provides atonement for past transgressions (although he holds the common Christian view that it does so), but that by sharing in Christ's death, one dies to the power of sin or to the old aeon, with the result that one belongs to God. The transfer is not only from the uncleanness of idolatry and sexual immorality to cleanness and holiness, but from one lordship to another.'[88]

So we can clinch this assessment of Paul's understanding of the death of Jesus in this vivid passage from Romans chapter 6,

> 'Are we to continue in sin that grace may abound? By no means! How can we who died to sin still live in it? Do you not know that all of us who have been baptized into Christ Jesus were baptized into his death? We were buried therefore with him by baptism into death, so that as Christ was raised from the dead by the glory of the Father, we too might walk in newness of life.
>
> For if we have been united with him in a death like his, we shall certainly be united with him in a resurrection like his. We know that our old self was crucified with him so that the sinful body might be destroyed, and we might no longer be enslaved to

---

[88] E. P. Sanders, *Paul and Palestinian Judaism*, SCM, 1977, pages 467-468, (the author's emphasis).

sin. For he who has died is freed from sin. But if we have died with Christ, we believe that we shall also live with him. For we know that Christ being raised from the dead will never die again; death no longer has dominion over him. The death he died he died to sin, once for all, but the life he lives he lives to God. So you also must consider yourselves dead to sin and alive to God in Christ Jesus. (Romans 6:1-11)

As Christians we participate now in the risen Lord. That is the gospel as Paul sees it and while Paul rarely refers to the facts of Jesus' life he was surely aware that Jesus, in his life, was drawing people to himself to share in his life in God in all the ways that the gospels portray.

During the early years of the infant church, the Jewish Christian disciples must have been perceptively aware of their history as a Jewish nation that had failed God and that Jesus had indeed, in some way, put that right. Indeed, it could be reasonably argued that the human race has a corporate 'conscience' that something has gone wrong in the history of the race that we cannot put right on our own initiative. So the Gentiles, hearing Paul's call to leave their false gods would realise that they needed to follow without hesitation the Lord of glory who died for them and who is now their Lord. But both Jewish Christians and Gentile Christians were still aware of a sinful nature which 'clings so closely' in this life. Indeed, at the close of the first century, the problem of sins committed after baptism became a real problem for some of the new Christian communities.[89]

---

[89] See Hermas, *Similitudes 7*, in Lightfoot, *The Apostolic Fathers*, Macmillan, 1898, page 452: 'Thinkest thou that the sins of those who repent are forgiven forthwith? Certainly not; but the person who repents must torture his own soul, and must be thoroughly humble in his every action, and be
(continued...)

But the common failure to live up to a standard of truth in daily life is not to be confused with the Pauline statement that Jesus died 'for our sins'. Since the third century the passion and death of Jesus has so often been misinterpreted simply because we find it hard to accept the gospel that in that death the grace and love of God has been once and for all manifested in the death and resurrection of Jesus and is offered freely to us all. We shall see how eventually, on account of wrong ideas of Jesus' death, it was thought proper to offer the sacrifice of Jesus continually in one way or another, either in a form of words or in the offering of eucharist.

From the 2nd to the 16th Century

In the following three centuries there appeared to be no great need to construct a theory of why Christ died 'for us'. Neither the 'apologies' of the second century theologians nor the accounts of Christian worship that we can discern from the little that has come to light from the third century, is there any great highlighting of the once-for-all death of Jesus. Possibly the risk of martyrdom, every now and again, for any who were known to be Christians, helped to keep in balance the crucifixion/resurrection faith handed down to them. One might say that there was a certain 'innocence' about the first two centuries which contrasts with the anxiety shown in the centuries following Cyprian.

In the second century, Irenaeus (130-202) made some positive

---

[89](...continued)
afflicted with all the divers kinds of affliction; and if he endure the afflictions which come upon him, assuredly he who created all things and endowed them with power will be moved with compassion and will bestow some remedy.'

remarks in the course of his refutation of Gnostic heresies. In particular the idea that in Jesus all the ages of humanity were recapitulated and reformed in the new creation of the crucifixion/resurrection of Jesus -

> '... he recapitulated in himself the long line of the human race, procuring for us salvation thus summarily, so that what we had lost in Adam, that is, being in the image and like ness of God, that we should regain in Christ Jesus.'

and -

> '... the Lord declares himself to be Son of man, because he recapitulates in himself the original man who was the source from which sprang the race fashioned after woman; that as through the conquest of man our race went down to death, so through the victory of man we might ascend to life.'[90]

It might be said that this acceptance of the literal 'Adam' is the first, and last, good use of it in Christian history!

However, Origen (182-251) proposed that the death of Christ was a 'ransom' paid to the devil but that it was a supreme act of self sacrifice on the part of Jesus and an example to everyone else. Later, Gregory of Nyssa (c335-394) thought up the idea that Christ, the Lord in human flesh, was a 'bait' to deceive the devil who swallowed the body of Jesus only to be snared by the hidden 'hook' of the divinity, like a fish, and was destroyed. These and other like 'snares' of atonement theories were repeated by Pope Leo, Gregory the Great and Augustine in various ways and are like debris littering the floor of the Christian church down the ages.

It was left to Anselm (1033-1109) to produce the theory which

---

[90] Irenaeus, Adv. Haer. III. xviii & V. xxi.1 in Henry Bettenson, *Documents of the Christian Church*, Oxford, 1943, pages 42-43.

still has an effect today. According to Anselm, God became man because of the disobedience of man, in order that by the obedience of the God Man, man might be redeemed. For man was made for blessedness but he has forfeited this right by sin. (In what follows I give excerpts from Anselm's work, set out in lines for greater clarity).

> 'To sin is to fail to give to God his due, that is, righteousness, or rectitude of will.
>
> It is not enough simply to restore what has been taken away; but in consideration of the insult offered, more than what was taken away must be rendered back. This is satisfaction.
>
> To remit sin without satisfaction would be simply to abstain from punishing it ... God cannot properly leave anything uncorrected in his kingdom.
>
> It is necessary therefore, that either the honour taken away should be repaid, or punishment should be inflicted.' (Anselm, Cur Deus Homo, Book I, xi, xii)
>
> 'Satisfaction cannot be made unless there be some One able to pay to God for man's sin something greater than all that is beside God ... God himself ... then necessarily One must make it who is both God and man.
>
> But death Christ was in no way bound to suffer, having never sinned. So death was an offering that He could make as of free will, and not of debt ...
>
> What greater mercy can be conceived than that God the Father

should say to the sinner - condemned to eternal torment, and unable to redeem himself - "Receive my only Son, and offer him for thyself," while the Son himself said, "Take me, and redeem thyself."

And what greater justice than that One who receives a payment far exceeding the amount due, should, if it be paid with a right intention, remit all that is due?' (Anselm, Cur Deus Homo, Book II, vi, xi and xx) [91]

The background to this extraordinary theory is possibly the feudalism of the time, in the relation of a contract between king and subjects, and in the juridical, penitential system of the West.[92] However, Anselm was heir also to a literal understanding of the Genesis story of the Fall, to the possibilities of eternal punishment for the unrepentant sinner and to ideas of a God who was impassible. Thomas Aquinas followed Anselm's theory but in a less extreme form, wishing rather to see the satisfaction made by Christ as the obedience of love. So by the end of the Middle Ages, in the Council of Trent, it was stated that 'Christ merited justification for us, and by his most holy passion on the wood of the cross made satisfaction to God the Father.'[93] The Church of England produced an account not very different from the Roman Catholic Church in

---

[91] Anselm, *Cur Deus Homo*, ibid. pages 193-195.

[92] But see David Brown's article, *Anselm on atonement* in *The Cambridge Companion to Anselm*, edited by Brian Davies and Brian Leftow, Cambridge, 2004, pages 279-298. Brown seeks to correct modern misinterpretation of Anselm's thought particularly in relation to the feudal background of the times.

[93] Council of Trent Session vi.c.7, quoted in J. K. Mozley, *The Doctrine of the Atonement*, Duckworth, 1953 [1915], page 183.

Atonement and the Eucharist

Article 2 of the 39 Articles -

'... [Christ, very God and very Man] truly suffered, was crucified, dead and buried, to reconcile his Father to us, and to be a sacrifice, not only for original guilt, but also for all actual sins of men.'

The 1662 Book of Common Prayer rite for Holy Communion also reflects this mediaeval outlook. The prayer of oblation includes the following phrases,

> 'Almighty God ... who of thy tender mercy didst give thine only Son Jesus Christ to suffer death upon the cross for our redemption; who made there ... a full, perfect and sufficient sacrifice, oblation and satisfaction for the sins of the whole world ...'

The 'sacrifice of the mass', representing an offering of Christ in and through the bread and wine had been removed, but the Anselmian ideas remain.

So it was quite in line with these ideas that Mrs Alexander could write the hymn we have already quoted,

> 'There was no other good enough
> to pay the price of sin ...';

and also William Shirley (1725-86),

> 'Here I stay, for ever viewing
> Mercy streaming in his blood,
> Precious drops, my soul bedewing,
> Plead and claim my peace with God.'

The 19th century still fostered the penal and substitutionary accounts of Christ's death, and these continue to our own time. But, as we have seen, they are not to be found in the New Testament writings but can only be wrenched out of them to fit our own preconceptions. Again, it is easy to abstract the emphasis often placed on the 'cross' by New Testament writers from the person of Jesus whose whole life was a giving to others. So, as Paul said,

> 'the word of the cross is folly to those who are perishing, but to us who are being saved it is the power of God ... a stumbling block to Jews and folly to Gentiles, but to those who are called, both Jews and Greeks, Christ the power of God and the wisdom of God..' 1Corinthians 1:18-24)

The preaching of Jesus as the crucified and vindicated Saviour is the truth of the gospel, i.e. the word of the cross. But a focus purely on the 'cross' alone, or a hypothetical 'payment' or 'deal' with God is not the gospel but a misunderstanding.

One wonders, too, whether the idea that the death of Jesus was part of the 'plan' of God, as set out in some parts of scripture, can ever be accepted today. So Peter is recorded as saying in Acts that Jesus was 'delivered up according to the definite plan and foreknowledge of God' (Acts 2:23). Perhaps one cannot know the 'mind' of God so clearly in terms of prophetic hindsight?[94] Looking back to our summary of God's 'possibilities', in terms of his

---

[94] 'Why did Christ die? ... because of human sin. This is an answer which we find stressed in the gospels, which emphasize the responsibility of Jesus' contemporaries for his death. But at a deeper level, we can give an answer which seems to be in direct contradiction to it: Jesus died because it was the will of God that he should die.' Morna D. Hooker, *Not Ashamed of the Gospel*, Paternoster Press, 1994, pages 15-19.

relationship with us, it may be more thoughtful to posit his going along with us in our need, even in this extreme need of a reconciliation of humanity, and the creation of new life in and through the personality of Jesus. In respect indeed of Jesus himself, all things point to a step by step, God-with-us approach rather than a pre-determined plan laid out in the mind of God. David Pailin has observed,

> ' ... Atonement with God comes through an existentially powerful and transformative perception that God suffers agony over the stupidity and cruelty in human behaviour and longs to lure human beings to see what is really good. So far, then, as the doctrine of atonement is understood in terms of models which imply that something has to be done if an offended God is to be able to be 'at one' with human beings, it rests on a misunderstanding ... It is time for believers and theologians to grow beyond many of the traditional doctrines of atonement as they seek to apprehend and interpret certain aspects of the Christian faith. Indeed, its basic demand is that Christian believers and theologians should take radically seriously the insight into the divine nature presented by the life and death of Jesus and not distort it by interpreting it in terms of sub-Christian views of God. As Alfred North Whitehead suggested, Christian theology should be formed by 'the brief Galilean vision' of God as operating 'in quietness ... by love' rather than by an image of 'the ruling Caesar, or the ruthless moralist, or the unmoved mover' (Whitehead 1978: 342f) - or, one might add, a touchy and pernickety fusspot.' [95]

---

[95] D. A. Pailin, *The Doctrine of the Atonement: Does it rest on a misunderstanding?*, in Probing the Foundations, Pharos, 1994, pages 178-

We shall be seeing later how important it is to always be keeping in mind the real and actual possibilities of a God who is personal, gracious and free.

Eucharistic worship and the death of Christ [96]

Ever since the late fourth century the eucharist has been connected with the death of Christ. This continues today in the liturgical renewal that has been taking place for the past half century. In this section I shall be looking at the first four centuries to find out why this came about. There are difficulties doing this as the eucharist was not written down until the late fourth century and all that we have are the discursive commentaries and letters of individuals beginning with Justin in the middle of the second century. It was expected that the presiding person would extemporize in prayer. But there is sufficient evidence to allow us to judge how the early Christians appeared to be thinking about the community meal and the command of Jesus, contained in the account of the Last Supper in Luke, and Paul's appeal to the tradition which he had received, to 'remember me'. It is worth while noting at the outset that Jesus apparently commanded a remembrance not of his death but of himself. What did that mean for the Christian church in the first three centuries and when and why did the later idea of the eucharist as a memorial of the crucifixion come about?

Because the writing of the gospels spanned the last fifty years of

---

[95](...continued)
188.

[96] For the details in this section I am indebted to Paul F. Bradshaw's two books: *The Search for the Origins of Christian Worship*, Second Edition, SPCK, 2002, (*Search*) and *Eucharistic Origins*, SPCK, 2004, (*Origins*).

the first century it had been taken for granted by many scholars that the Institution narrative had been taken from the actual practice of the worship of the Christian communities in Palestine and Syria during that period. However, from the evidence that we have, the institution narratives didn't begin to appear in eucharistic material until the late fourth century and then they were apparently used more as theological catechesis rather than as part of the eucharistic celebration as we have known it, acting in a consecratory function as they have done throughout the centuries since that time. So the narratives of the institution appear to be mainly descriptive, rather than reflections of actual eucharistic practice. It had also been supposed that the actual meal, which at the Last Supper was preceded by the blessing over the bread and followed by that of the cup, had disappeared before the gospels were written, or even before Paul wrote 1 Corinthians in early 53-4. From the orthodox, liturgical point of view, the early removal of this meal or agape would mean that our liturgical tradition of the eucharist went right back to the early first century, to the apostles or even to Jesus himself. But there is no actual evidence that there was at any time a deliberate separation of the meal or agape from the eucharistic rite until the fourth century when there was a surge of people entering the church after the peace made by Constantine, when larger congregations required more space than the large houses which appear to have been used in the previous two centuries. We need first of all to look at the gospel narratives of the Institution and then at the late 1st or early 2nd century Didache which is possibly a eucharistic service.

The narratives of the Institution, inserted into the accounts of the Last Supper, vary in detail and the hypothetical reconstruction of how they came to be as they are in the gospels is very complicated. This is the account in Mark:

'And as they were eating, he took bread, and blessed, and broke it, and gave it to them, and said, "Take; this is my body." And he took a cup, and when he had given thanks he gave it to them, and they all drank of it. And he said to them, "This is my blood of the covenant, which is poured out for many. Truly, I say to you, I shall not drink again of the fruit of the vine until that day when I drink it new in the kingdom of God."' (Mark 14:22-25)

Matthew has a similar account with slight variations and the addition of, 'for the forgiveness of sins' after 'poured out for many' (Matthew 26:28) However, Luke has an account with two cups, the first before the bread,

'And he took a cup, and when he had given thanks he said, "Take this, and divide it among yourselves; for I tell you that from now on I shall not drink of the fruit of the vine until the kingdom of God comes."' (Luke 22:17-18)

and then,

'He took bread, and when he had given thanks he broke it and gave it to them, saying, "This is my body which is given for you. Do this in remembrance of me." And likewise the cup after supper, saying, "This cup which is poured out for you is the new covenant in my blood."' (Luke 22:19-20)[97]

It is only Luke who has the command, 'do this in remembrance of me' after the bread and this occurs also in Paul's account, with the command added after the cup also,

---

[97] There is also the 'shorter account' in some manuscripts in Luke which omits verses 19b-20, so omitting the second cup and also the command to remember.

Atonement and the Eucharist

> 'I received from the Lord what I also delivered to you, that the Lord Jesus on the night when he was betrayed took bread, and when he had given thanks, he broke it, and said, "This is my body which is for you. Do this in remembrance of me." In the same way also the cup, after supper, saying, "This cup is the new covenant in my blood. Do this, as often as you drink it, in remembrance of me." For as often as you eat this bread and drink the cup, you proclaim the Lord's death until he comes.'(1 Corinthians 11:23-26)

The final sentence is unique to Paul and reflects, (as we have noted above), an eschatological understanding of the crucifixion, to the effect that at the celebration of the eucharist it is not the past event of the death in the passion of Jesus that is being proclaimed, but the death as the eschatological event which inaugurated the new covenant.[98]

There seem to have been at least two sources for these accounts, the one in Mark, followed by Matthew which do not have the 'remembrance' command and Luke's account with Paul which does. Perhaps the first originating from Jerusalem and the other from Antioch in Syria. So how did these accounts get into the gospel traditions at all? It has been speculated that there were oral traditions of the sayings which were circulating but never used as part of the worshipping traditions of the communities of the first three centuries. As source material, they would easily have been taken and put into the last Supper narratives. As we shall be seeing, this would account for the sparse citations in the following centuries, lacking 'any reference to the occasion and context in which the sayings of Jesus were uttered or to the ritual shape of the Last Supper, and even any of the interpretive phrases connecting body and blood to

---

[98] Jeremias, *The Eucharistic Words of Jesus*, SCM, 1966, page 253.

the covenant or giving sacrificial meaning to them, such as 'which is for you' or 'which is poured out for many for the forgiveness if sins.'[99]

Quite different from these relatively sophisticated accounts of the Institution narratives is the late first century - early part of the second century text of the Didache. Found in 1883 it has been the cause of much controversy as to what purpose it served. Was it a eucharist? Its very simple shape seems to deny it a place in the various eucharistic 'rites' of the first three centuries. It has no sacrificial connotations or link to the death of Christ, has no hint of the words of the Institution narratives and begins with the cup. Yet its simplicity has been recognized by some to be a eucharist perhaps of the type celebrated by the infant community as described in Acts,

> 'breaking bread in their homes, they partook of food with glad and generous hearts, praising God and having favour with all the people, (Acts 3:46-47),

if 'breaking bread' in the Acts' context was an early eucharist. In that case, as has been pointed out it may have belonged to a type of 'free' and joyful eucharist as contrasted perhaps with the Pauline's apparent emphasis on the death of Jesus? But we may be questioning that description later.

The Didache

> *Concerning the thanksgiving, give thanks thus:*
> First concerning the cup:

---

[99] *Origins*, page 14.

'We give thanks to you, our Father, for the holy vine of David your child, which you have made known to us through Jesus your child; glory to you for evermore.

Concerning the broken bread:

We give thanks to you, our Father, for the life and knowledge which you have made known to us through Jesus your child; glory to you for evermore.
As this broken bread was scattered upon the mountains and having been gathered together became one, so may your church be gathered together from the ends of the earth into your kingdom; for yours is the glory and the power; through Jesus Christ for evermore ...

You, Almighty Master, created all things for the sake of your name and gave food and drink to humans for enjoyment, that they might give thanks to you; but to us you have granted spiritual food and drink and eternal life through Jesus your child ...

May grace come, and this world pass away. Amen.
Hosanna to the God of David.
If anyone is holy, let him come; if anyone is not, let him repent.
Marana tha. Amen.'[100]

In a later chapter of the Didache there is a reference to the spiritual sacrifice of worship along the lines of that in Malachi 1:11 and 1:14,
'In every place and time offer me a pure sacrifice; for I am a great king, says the Lord, and my name is wonderful among the

---

[100] *Origins*, pages 24-25.

nations.'

This is apparently the first Christian use of the text of Malachi and may be the first text to maintain that Christian worship is a sacrifice.

From the time of Justin in the middle of the second century until the late fourth century there is quite a considerable variation in references to the eucharist in the scattered material which has come down to us. This may be due to the fact that until the time of Cyprian in the middle of the third century, the gospels and Paul's letters are by no means known everywhere. There were also, apparently, signs of eucharists with bread, (following the Emmaus incident of the 'breaking of the bread'?) and no cup; and eucharists with only water and bread. It has been pointed out that the normal family would generally have bread, salt and water for a meal and as the eucharist was part of this 'substantial', proper meal, there would have been no wine available.[101] Apart from Ignatius of Antioch, at the turn of the first century, there is little said about the eucharist as a sacrifice until Cyprian in 250.

So Ignatius writes to the Philadelphians,

> 'Be ye careful therefore to observe one eucharist (for there is one flesh of our Lord Jesus Christ and one cup unto union in His blood; there is one altar, as there is one bishop, together with the presbytery and the deacons my fellow-servants), that whatsoever ye do, ye may do it after God.'[102]

Ignatius was of course on his way to his martyrdom in Rome and the thought of 'sacrifice' is always in his thoughts and letters. He is also the only one to mention 'altar', which is very unusual at this

---

[101] Andrew McGowan, *Ascetic Eucharists: Food and Drink in early Christian Ritual Meals*, Oxford, 1998; and *Origins*, pages 51-55.

[102] J. B. Lightfoot, *The Apostolic Fathers*, MacMillan, 1898, page 154.

time. The reference to the 'flesh' of Jesus, seems to mean that he did not know the synoptic gospels but only St John, '... except you eat my flesh ...' (John 6:53).

Justin (c 100/114 c. 162/168) also uses 'flesh' instead of body in his account of the eucharist,

> ' ... we have been taught that blessed by the prayer of his Word, and from which our blood and flesh by transmutation are nourished, is the flesh and blood of that Jesus who was made flesh ... For the apostles ... delivered unto us ... that Jesus took bread, and when he had given thanks, said, "Do this in remembrance of me, this is my body." and that, after the same manner, having taken the cup and given thanks, he said, "This is my blood."'[103]

Justin also provides an outline of the form the eucharist took in his time at Rome,

> 'There is then brought to the president of the brethren bread and a cup of wine mixed with water; and he taking them, gives praise and glory to the Father of the universe, through the name of the Son and of the Holy Ghost, and gives thanks at considerable length for our being counted worthy to receive these things at his hands..'[104]

Irenaeus (175-185) writes about the church offering a pure oblation to God, 'offering the first fruits of his own created things' and quotes Paul's reference to the gifts brought by Epaphroditus. With

---

[103] Roberts and Donaldson, *The Ante-Nicene Fathers*, Volume 1, Eerdmans, 1884, page 185.

[104] ibid. page 185.

this reference it seems that the New Testament writings were becoming more widely known towards the end of the second century. Irenaeus writes also of the eucharist as being nourishment for human flesh as well as an offering to God,

> 'For as the bread, which is produced from the earth, when it receives the invocation of God, is no longer common bread, but the Eucharist, consisting of two realities, earthly and heavenly; so also our bodies, when they receive the Eucharist, are no longer corruptible, having the hope of the resurrection to eternity ... Now we make offering to him, not as though he stood in need of it, but rendering thanks for his gift, and thus sanctifying what has been created.'[105]

Paul Bradshaw remarks, '...second century Christianity, at least attested by its two great theological writers Justin and Irenaeus, does not seem to know the notion of 'memorial sacrifice' as articulated by later theologians.'[106] However, with Cyprian (martyred in 258), there is a change. The threat of martyrdom was a live issue at the time in North Africa, and that together with the greater use being made of the New Testament Institution narratives as Scripture at the time, may have combined to alter the perception of the Eucharist. The bread and the cup are said to be offered in remembrance of the passion of Jesus. In a letter Cyprian says, 'we make mention of his passion in all sacrifices, for the Lord's passion is the sacrifice we offer.'[107] There was also a change in the way the eucharist was thought of. With Cyprian the eucharist is beginning to be thought

---

[105] ibid. page 468.

[106] *Origins*, page 84.

[107] Cyprian, *Ep.* 63,17 in *Origins*, page 110.

of as being made by the priest for the people rather than being the action of the people as a whole. So, Cyprian writes in Ep. 67, of 'the honour of the priesthood',[108] and 'just as Christ offered himself as a sacrifice, so does the priest offer the church's sacrifice in memory of him.'[109]

In these first 250 years it probably depended a great deal on where you lived and what were the interactions with the local people and circumstances as to how you viewed the eucharist. It might be quite different being in Rome rather than in Lyons or Carthage. In Carthage, as we have just noticed, there was the danger of persecution and also the problem of the restoration of lapsed presbyters in a recent persecution. Apart from that there was presumably quite a difference if you were African rather than European, even at that time. Cyprian comes across with quite a lot of 'heat' in his correspondence. In Gaul there was the problem of Gnosticism against which Irenaeus has to defend what he sees as the main understanding of Christian truth in his time, and Lyons was quite a different environment from North African Carthage. It is also evident that the gospel accounts of the Institution were not seen as a form of ritual. Paul, for instance, is not writing to the Corinthians saying that his account of the Institution was a blueprint for the celebration of the eucharist. Rather his aim was to convince the Corinthians that they needed to look to their behaviour at the Lord's Supper, to regard those who were poorer, both in the main meal and the eucharist. There is, in the evidence that has come down to us, a great variety of ways of celebrating the eucharist, the main unifying link being the participation in the Lord who was crucified and was now with them, the vindicated, risen Lord.

---

[108] *A new Eusebius*, edited by J. Stevenson, SPCK, 1974, page 250.

[109] *Origins*, page 111.

A hundred years after the death of Cyprian we find that in the mid fourth century, in the Mystagogical lectures attributed to Cyril of Jerusalem, there are several ideas which must have been developing before and after the peace of Constantine in 313. So we find in the commentary on the liturgy the ideas that were later to become normal,

'after the spiritual sacrifice, the bloodless worship, has been completed, we beseech God, over that sacrifice of propitiation, for peace ...'[110] and, '... we offer Christ slain for our sins.'

There is no narrative of Institution mentioned in the lectures, so we do not know whether it was included in the eucharistic prayer in Jerusalem or not. The idea of the eucharist as a sacrifice, from the earliest ideas of an offering of the bread and cup or of the fruits of the earth, will develop from now on into a definite connection with the passion and death of Christ. So John Chrysostom (347-407) can speak of the 'dreadful sacrifice', of the 'fearful moment' when the mysteries are accomplished, and of the 'terrible and awesome table' that should only be approached in fear and trembling.[111] While a great deal of Chrysostom's language was hortatory, making the attempt to inculcate the right attitude of mind in a congregation at Constantinople which seems to have been less than devout, as far as the bishop was concerned, there was obviously the chance that such phrases would pass into the future with distinct theological overtones.

---

[110] *Mystagogical Catechesis*, 5.6-9 in *Origins*, page 148.
[111] *Origins*, page 141.

The Commemoration of Jesus in the Eucharist today

Redemption, sacrifice, satisfaction, propitiation, expiation - these are some of the terms we have come across in the history of theological ideas of the death of Christ. By the end of the fourth century some of them were also being used in the commemoration of Christ in the eucharistic celebrations of the church. While it may be true that coming out into the open after the peace of Constantine in 313 was a challenge to the Christian church to be at least as 'religious' as the pagan rites which had altars, a priesthood and sacrifices, the roots of these ideas were already apparent a hundred years previously in the North African church at Carthage. The change from the early second century rite of the Didache and even compared with that of the second century main witnesses such as Justin and Irenaeus, is quite significant. Can we account for this in any way? One reason, as we have already mentioned, was that the texts of the synoptic gospels were becoming more widely known. But the further away one got from the early Christian communities of the second half of the first century, when the gospels were written, the more possible was it to take those texts literally. The human face and the nuances behind the texts was probably by now no longer visible. But even if the Institution narrative, from the end of the fourth century onwards, determined the meaning of the rite, that text specified the remembrance of Jesus, as we have noticed, and not the remembrance of his death. So the text did not, in effect, influence the growth of the introduction of 'atonement' theology into the eucharist. There must have been other influences which would eventually lead to the use of the eucharist from early mediaeval times as a continual pleading again and again of Jesus' death 'for our sins'.

One of the reasons may be the fact that from the fifth century onwards, Europe and the Eastern part of the Empire, was more and more at risk from the huge wave of invasions that swept over the countries and eventually brought them into three centuries of bondage. It is true that the barbarians were often Christians of an Arian lineage but life was becoming, in the dissolution of the Pax Romana, dangerous and fragile. What could be more tempting than to see that in Jesus' own sacrifice, there was the option to make it a recurring plea before God for the vital needs of the moment? Such ideas grow exponentially in such a soil. We do not need to introduce the wrong sort of comparison with post-modernity, and to call those centuries 'primitive' in their understanding of the gospels. They were highly educated and sophisticated people but probably more vulnerable than we can possibly understand in face of the threats facing their civilisation. Even when Europe was released from it's bondage in the mid eleventh century, conditions were not ripe for what we might call a more humane understanding of the gospel writers' account of the death of Jesus. Even Anselm was answering the need for an articulate account, for his times, for an atonement theory.

Another reason could be that Paul was now being used much more in statements about the death of Jesus. Many of these can be taken to mean something entirely different when taken out of their contexts, as we have seen. One example is the often quoted phrase from Galatians,

'... far be it from me to glory except in the cross of our Lord Jesus Christ, by which the world has been crucified to me, and I to the world.' (Galatians 6:14)

This comes in the context of Paul's rebuttal of the Galatians apparent desire that circumcision should be part of the Christian's commitment. It is not a statement about the cross on its own being the centrality of the gospel, but an insistence that in Jesus' death we have all been taken away from the law of Torah and Jewish custom into the freedom of the sons of God. As Paul says earlier in Galatians, 'For as many of you as were baptized into Christ have put on Christ,' and, 'For freedom Christ has set us free.' And it is worthwhile repeating again what Paul writes in 2 Corinthians, showing his total grasp of the gospel that is revealed in the person of Jesus and not simply in the death,

> 'Therefore, if any one is in Christ, he is a new creation; the old has passed away, behold, the new has come. All this is from God, who through Christ reconciled us to himself and gave us the ministry of reconciliation; that is, in Christ God was reconciling the world to himself, not counting their trespasses against them, and entrusting to us the message of reconciliation. (2 Corinthians 5:17-19)

Remembering Sanders insistence that Jesus' death was mainly about taking us out of the allegiance of the aeon of paganism and the false gods to that of the true God we might also quote Käsemann's comments on Paul's problems with the celebration of the eucharist at Corinth in 1 Corinthians 11:23-34

> 'The Apostle is maintaining against every possible magical, metaphysical or mystical misinterpretation that it is the Kyrios himself in his self-manifestation who is dealing with us; and dealing with us in such a way as to lay hold on our will, lay claim to our obedience and set himself over us as indeed our Lord.'[112]

---

[112] Ernst Käsemann, *The Pauline Doctrine of the Lord's Supper*, page 134, in Essays on New Testament Themes, SCM Press, Studies in Biblical Theology No 41, 1964.

The understanding that the risen Lord is present at the eucharist, in advance of anything that we do or say at the service, underlines the proposal that it is the person of Jesus who should be the central concern in our celebration of eucharist. There is the need to sweep away the mist, and misunderstanding, surrounding the phraseology of 'sins' used so often in eucharistic services, however pressing those culpas may reasonably be; (we do need to repent, that is sure). It may be said in parenthesis, that the later fourth century was also the time when, with the influx of new Christians, there was also the possibility of pagan ideas influencing the eucharist. The idea, for instance that the sacrament could be a sort of talisman against evil or disease is well documented. Augustine was concerned that Monica, his mother, used the sacrament in this way.

The opinions of 'atonement' from the past 1600 years have been repeated in the theological and liturgical text books up to the present day. Constant reference to the dying and the cross is, in the New Testament, only the necessary identification of Jesus as Son of man, who was crucified. It is a reference to the action that happened in the past, once and for all. The modern Anglican and Roman Catholic eucharists use language which speaks of Jesus' offering for our sins and phrases such as - pleading his sacrifice, the merits of his death, faith in his blood, of the satisfaction Jesus made, giving him to die upon the cross - all of which, taken out of their context in the New Testament arguments, are part of a mediaeval outlook. Some such sentence as , 'Through the life, death and resurrection of Jesus, you restored humanity, offering peace and freedom to all people', would recover for worship the understanding of God and Christ working together in love to reconcile us.

The gospel speaks of the person of Jesus who has led us out to this new 'land', the land of the present kingdom of God which he inaugurated in his life. Announced at the outset of Mark's gospel, Jesus came to inaugurate the kingdom of his Father among us.

Should we not then be looking for ways in which, in the presence of the risen Lord with us at eucharist, we may be able to phrase our 'remembrance' in such a way that reflects the New Testament understanding? The earliest eucharists which appear to have been cast on the model of a festive, joyous occasion - a gathering of thanksgiving with the Lord - could provide that reality of faith for the present day worshipper who is looking for that light of the glory that can be seen only in the face of Jesus - for, 'we all, with unveiled face, beholding the glory of the Lord, are being changed into his likeness from one degree of glory to another; for this comes from the Lord who is the Spirit.' (2 Corinthians 3:18)

CHAPTER 8

Remembrance in the Eucharist

In this chapter I shall be concentrating on the meaning of the Greek word for remembrance, *anamnesis*. We shall look first of all at the ordinary, human understanding of remembering. Then we shall turn to the idea of remembrance proposed by Jesus for the celebration of the eucharist. Finally we shall investigate religious theories of remembrance proposed by some liturgical scholars.

Memory is the greatest asset we have but, as Lady Macbeth says, it can be fuddled and can lie,

' ... will I with wine and wassail so convince
That memory, the warder of the brain,
Shall be a fume and the receipt of reason
A limbec only.'(Macbeth, Act1, Scene 7)[113]

Memory enables us, in a sort of way, to re-live episodes from the past. There is a reality in recalling old activities with friends, or events which made a great impression on us. Daily life has a larger context than the present moment. Snippets of information from the past come to mind which, unlike perhaps the data we accumulated for examinations, remain with us always. Friends come momentarily to 'life' when we think of them. But memory also seems to have a healing mode when painful memories appear to have been erased as we move on into the future of our lives. But what is the substance of memories? Jung would no doubt be willing to tell us but it is in no way an essential part of my thesis to wander into a psychological mode. Suffice it to say that there is a measure of reality in these

---

[113] William Shakespeare, *The Complete Works*, General Editors: Stanley Wells and Gary Taylor, Clarendon, 1988, page 971.

'remembrances' which we can respect and see as a part of our journey in daily living. It is vital of course to see that, however much we might like to, remembrances can never 'bring back' the events we review in our minds. To that extent they are 'phantoms', good or bad, and if bad then we can get help to see how they can be neutralised.

There is much in folk religion that relies on memories of the past, particularly in the realm of a sort of corporate memory of the tribe. Out of that have come rituals, in primitive societies, which depend upon keeping individuals anchored to the past. In this respect the work of anthropologists such as Mircea Eliade, claim to have unearthed the rituals of primitive societies. Eliade points out that recovery of the primordial events enshrined in the 'myth' of the people is a vital matter. To recover in reality the primordial time of their beginnings there was the need to re-live, to re-enact the myth in a regular, cyclic rhythm. Most particularly, by the sacred meal the corporate life of the community was expressed and the primordial myth recovered through ritual re-enactment.

> 'In religion as in magic, the periodic recurrence of anything signifies primarily that a mythical time is made present and then used indefinitely. Every ritual has the character of happening now, at this very moment. The time of the event that the ritual commemorates or re-enacts is made present, "re-presented" so to speak, however far back it may have been in ordinary reckoning.'[114]

---

[114] *Patterns in Comparative Religion*, Sheed & Ward,(1953), 1993, pages 392-393. It is worth pointing out that Eliade's theory, although espoused in different forms by some liturgists, does not provide any foundation for the Christian eucharist.

This 're-enactment' or 'making-present' of an event in the past belongs rather to fantasy than to real life, at least in the civilised world. We shall be seeing, however, that something of this idea has been imported into liturgical theories of what 'happens' at eucharist in recent times, to the overturning of the normal understanding of the use of memory.

Jesus and Remembrance

The gospel, as I have mentioned several times already, is the gospel of Jesus who was crucified and was raised. One cannot discuss the command 'do this in remembrance of me' except in relation to the fact that Jesus is alive. So he is present to the world and to us as the risen Lord; present, that is, in a transcendent presence. We have no physical contact with him. But as in the presence of a friend we use our mind and memory to maintain converse, so we are to keep Jesus, the Lord, in mind; remember him as present in our daily life and in particular as we celebrate the Christian Eucharist.

The acted symbolism of bread and cup is quite a separate matter for it belongs to a particular moment in Jesus' life, prophetically showing forth his imminent death. As Xavier Léon-Dufour says,

> 'Even though the death is at first glance the centre of attention, it is in fact 'overridden' ... The community's future meals will not therefore have the limited function of enabling the faithful to be present to Christ's death, rather they will celebrate his new life with God ... it is the new relationship between Jesus and the disciples that takes priority.'[115]

---

[115] Xavier Léon-Dufour, *Sharing the Eucharistic Bread*, transl Matthew J. O'Connell, Paulist Press, New York, 1982, page 69.

In many ways Christian worship and prayer is totally different from anything that had gone on before. There was a sea change. Christian services are not 'rites' and prayer is not hammering at the doors of heaven. Jesus, the risen Lord and Master, is the centre of a response to God in a celebration which gives thanks with the present Lord for the new life which had been brought to our world and from that point to pray for the world before God. 'Remembering' is then the attitude of living in Christ now and seeing the passion and death as the fulcrum of this eschatological foretaste we now have of the future in God. We have noted that the first three centuries do not have a tradition of treating the eucharist as a memorial of Jesus' death until the time of Cyprian in the North African church.

Remembering Jesus is, however, for a Christian, not a perfunctory matter. It is a use of memory to access that point in our being and daily life where we have been united to Christ the Lord. It is not perfunctory because it is a daily ascesis to live at this level of being. Paul takes this for granted in that quotation we had previously from Romans 6, 'We were buried therefore with him by baptism into death, so that as Christ was raised from the dead by the glory of the Father, we too might walk in newness of life.' Like Jesus' death, our baptism was a 'once-for-all' action. So we may say that Jesus was appealing to the possibility of our responding to him through the normal, human faculty of our mind. There is nothing esoteric about remembering Jesus. It is the reality of living in Christ from second to second, and for this we need to use our minds and memory.

But this has been questioned by a long tradition that assumes that the risen Lord is absent from the world in which we live. If this is the case then we need, (this tradition says), some means of access to the events of the passion and death of Jesus, and to seek to have him present with us in our worship. 'Remembering' in this sense is not human memory dedicated to a commitment to discipleship with the risen Lord, but a 'technique' to connect us at the eucharist with either the crucified Lord or with the 'effects' of his passion so that he and they are no longer in the past but made present to us in our worship. This view is intimately connected with the ideas of atonement that we have been discussing. We need now to enter into a dialogue with these theories.

Theories of remembrance in the liturgy[116]

The most recent theory which is taught in all textbooks of liturgy is one that is based on the use of the Greek word anamnesis (remembrance) in the New Testament. This theory claims that anamnesis means, 'to "re-call" or to "re-present" before God an event in the past, so that it becomes here and now operative by its effects.'[117]

Dom Gregory Dix in his book, The Shape of the Liturgy, maintained that in our usage

> 'remembrance' or 'memorial' have the meaning only of mental recollection of something that is absent. So he wished to maintain that in antiquity there was a more dynamic understanding, '... we have to take account of the clear understanding then general in a largely Greek-speaking church of the word anamnesis as meaning a "re-calling" or "re-presenting" of a thing in such a way that it is not so much regarded as being "absent", as itself presently operative by its effects. This is a sense which the Latin memoria and its cognates do not adequately

---

[116] Some of the details of this section have appeared in my article in *Theology* Nov/Dec 2002 on pages 436-443.

[117] G. Dix, *The Shape of the Liturgy*, Dacre Press, 1945, page 161.

translate.'[118]

Dix is presumably referring to Plato's use of anamnesis as the recollection or recalling of knowledge in the immortal soul when it is repeatedly incarnated. But this referral to a Greek language understanding does not necessarily mean what the gospel writers intended in their commitment to the risen Lord in their communities. Dix goes on to apply this meaning to eucharist, 'It is in this active sense, therefore, of "re-calling" or "re-presenting" before God the sacrifice of Christ, and thus making it here and now operative by its effects in the communicants that the eucharist is regarded both by the New Testament and by second century writers as the anamnesis of the passion, or of the passion and resurrection combined.'[119]

Dix gives three texts in support of his anamnesis theory - Numbers 5:15; 1 Kings 17:18 & Hebrews 10:3-4. In these texts Dix wished to translate anamnesis as 're-call' but in fact the Hebrew lying behind the Septuagint text clearly means 'remembrance' in one form or another. For example,1 Kings 17:18 is translated by Dix as - "the widow of Sarepta complains that Elijah has come 'to "re-call" to (God's) remembrance my iniquity', and therefore her son has died."[120] In the NEB it is translated, 'What made you interfere, you man of God? You came here to bring my sins to light and kill my son.' *zkr* is the Hebrew for remembrance, meaning: remember, recall, call to mind. Here the hiphil of *zkr* [121], following the Hebrew, *rwn* (sin), is used in a technical sense meaning 'to accuse' before

---

[118] Dix, page 245.

[119] ibid. page 161.

[120] ibid. page 161.

[121] See Brown ,Driver & Briggs, Hebrew & English Lexicon, Oxford, 1906 pages 269-271.

God.[122] Westcott pointed out in his commentary on Hebrews 10:3-4 that eis tēn emēn anamnēsin meant in that passage 'a calling to mind of sins.'[123]

There appears to be no case for Dix's translation of the word. If one consults the dictionaries and lexicons, anamnesis, both in the Septuagint and in the New Testament, means 'remember', 'recollect'. So C. F. Evans, in his commentary on Luke, translates eis tēn emēn anamnēsin as 'have me in mind.'[124]

Linked with this conception of anamnesis as a 're-calling' of an event from the past is the notion that in the five occurrences of the word in the Septuagint[125] it reflects a Jewish sacrificial ritual. So Darwell Stone, after reviewing the evidence, concluded that,

> 'The word "memorial" naturally suggests, without actually necessitating, the sense of a sacrificial memorial before God; and that in the case of the institution of the Eucharist the probability of a sacrificial meaning is greatly strengthened by the use of the word "covenant" just before and by the sacrificial surroundings when our Lord spoke.'[126]

Stone was followed by others in the same vein and notably by Stephen Bedale in 1953 who concluded that 'the word anamnesis on each occasion of its use in the LXX has exclusively a "God-ward

---

[122] ibid. page 271.

[123] B. F. Westcott, *The Epistle to the Hebrews*, Macmillan & Co., 1892, pages 306-307.

[124] C. F. Evans, 'Luke', SCM, 1990, pages 790-791.

[125] Leviticus 24:7; Numbers 10:10; Psalm 38(LXX 37),1; Psalm 70(LXX 69),1; Wisdom 16:6.

[126] Darwell Stone, *A History of the Doctrine of the Holy Eucharist*, Longmans, Green & Co., 1909, Vol. 1, page 11.

Remembrance in the Eucharist

reference."'[127] However, D. R. Jones in an article on Anamnēsis in the LXX and the Interpretation of 1 Corinthians 11: 25, at the conclusion of his study of these and other passages says, '... the use of the word anamnēsis in the LXX involves too many ambiguities to provide authority for any particular interpretation of New Testament passages.[128] Jones also adds the comment of Buchanan Grey that 'all attempts to interpret the Lord's eis tēn emēn anamnēsin in the light of Jewish sacrificial ritual in any case fail to explain the emēn.'[129]

In the case of the second century writers to whom Dix appeals, it is well known that their expression of eucharist is quite realist. Ignatius, Justin and Irenaeus give clear instances of this usage.[130] So Justin says that the eucharist '... is the flesh and blood of that Jesus who was made flesh.' But none of the pre-Nicene writers put forward any theory of what they supposed was happening in eucharist. They were writing in response to challenges from gnostics and pagans and were simply concerned to state that the Christian eucharist was really about worship with the crucified and living Lord.

Since Dix it has become common to refer to what is claimed to be a Semitic usage of anamnesis in the first century. It has been maintained that in the celebration of Passover, the Jews of the first century and the Jews of today, make the events of the original Passover present by their remembrance of it. In fact the opposite is

---

[127] Stephen Bedale, *The Eucharistic Sacrifice*, Theology, lvi, No 398 (1953).

[128] Journal of Theological Studies,(JTS), N. S. Vol. VI, Pt 2, October 1955, page 183.

[129] Buchanan Grey, *Sacrifice in the Old Testament*, pp.395-6. (Quoted in D. R. Jones, op.cit. page 188).

[130] Ignatius to the Smyrnaeans, chapter 7, *Ante-Nicene Fathers*, Eerdmans, page 89; Justin, Apology, I, 66 in *A New Eusebius*, ed. J. Stephenson, SPCK, 1957; 6th impression 1974, pages 66-67; Irenaeus, Adv. Haer. V.2.3, ibid. page 124.

the truth about Passover.[131] It is as if they were there. As D. R. Davies says, 'Memory of a deliverance was central in the Jewish Passover.'[132] At a supper with lamb, unleavened bread and bitter herbs, they re-tell the events of Passover and re-enact the flight to freedom from slavery in Egypt and the crossing of the Red Sea. It is a time of great rejoicing and excitement, but it is not making the past event present.

Today the anamnesis theory appears in two forms. There are those who say that anamnesis means 'to make effective in the present an event in the past.' The Anglican-Roman Catholic International Commission (ARCIC) refers to it in that form, 'The notion of memorial as understood in the Passover celebration at the time of Christ - i.e. the making effective in the present of an event in the past ...'[133] (Which I have just shown to be not the case!)

There are others who contend that it means not simply to make a past event effective but actually to make the past event present. By making anamnesis, it is claimed, Christ, or the effects of his passion, will be actualised in eucharist. So J. D. Crichton maintained,

> 'Through making memorial of (the past events of God's saving mercy) we are asking that their saving power may be made present to us here and now. ... and because we do so according

---

[131] Cf the rabbinic teaching on the Passover, 'In every generation a man must so regard himself as if he came forth himself out of Egypt.'*Pes.* 10.5 Danby, *Mishnah*, page 151.(Quoted in C. P. M. Jones, *The Eucharist in the New Testament*, in *The Study of Liturgy*, SPCK, 1978, page 154).

[132] Cf *Haggadah*, (London, 1897) by A. A. Green, page 27, 'Now even though all of us were wise, all of us of great understanding, all of us learned as elders, all of us familiar with Scripture, it would still be our duty to tell again the story of the Exodus from Egypt ...' (Quoted in D. R. Davies, *Paul & Rabbinic Judaism*, SPCK, 1955, page 252).

[133] ARCIC, *The Final Report*, Eucharistic Doctrine, pages 14-15.

to the command of Christ ... Christ makes himself present in all his redeeming activity.'[134]

George Guiver CR, connects with the idea of primordial myth,

> 'The full meaning of the Greek word anamnesis is remembrance, done in such a way as to call forth the actual presence here and now of the person and deeds commemorated, in the kind of way that liturgical re-enactment of myths has always done.'[135]

Crichton also comments on the work of Dom Odo Casel on the Continent in promoting the view of the eucharist as 'mystery'.

> 'What then is the particular significance of the use of the word mystery in the liturgy? It is a link between the past and the present, or rather it looks to the past to recover the power of the primordial event and makes its power present in the here and now so that the worshiper can encounter the redeeming Christ.'

And more specifically, Crichton writes, '...by the liturgical mystery we are actualizing the past event, making it present ...'[136] (See the reference to the word *mystery* on page 140.)

It is noticeable that in these liturgical theories of what happens at eucharist, all the writers without exception begin, not from the person of Jesus as the New Testament authors express our relationship to him in discipleship, but from liturgical texts and biblical words forced into a ritual understanding. The result is that eucharist appears to be something that we must activate, according

---

[134]*The Study of Liturgy*, SPCK, 1978, page 26.

[135]*Company of Voices*, SPCK, 1988, page 9.

[136]*The Study of Liturgy*, SPCK, 1978, pages 13-14.

to a rite, rather than a response to the prevenient action of Christ in the Spirit as we come to respond to the Father in worship. Remembering our discussion about the characteristics of God, we have to ask, 'What sort of God is it who requires the worship envisaged by the anamnesis theory? Is it the Father of Jesus or a god of abstractions?'

By 1971 the anamnesis theory had become a common-place of liturgical understanding. So much so that it could be quoted in the ARCIC document on the Eucharist.[137] Despite complaints from some sources about the use of this theory, ARCIC gave no supporting evidence for its continued acceptance of it. But one phrase in the Elucidation of 1979 was revealing, which will take us back to Dix and the Shape of the Liturgy. ARCIC said, '(this use of the word) enables us to affirm a strong conviction of sacramental realism and to reject mere symbolism.'[138] It was Dix's conviction that the 'protestant' eucharist was simply a mental remembering of Jesus and his sacrifice, quite lacking any corporate action.

> 'The new (protestant conception)', he wrote, 'is of a strictly personal mental reflection upon (Christ's) action in the past. We cannot enter into it, since as a matter of history the passion is unique and finished...and the bread and wine need only be a "token".'[139]

We can reasonably conclude from these excerpts that the anamnesis theory, together with so-called 'sacramental realism', is clearly a reaction against what is styled 'mere remembrance' or 'mere symbolism'. It seems to have been accepted everywhere as a

---

[137] ARCIC, *The Final Report*, Eucharistic Doctrine, page 14.

[138] ARCIC, *Elucidation*, Eucharistic Doctrine, page 19.

[139] *The Shape of the Liturgy*, page 624.

replacement for the theory of 'transubstantiation' which had been the normal explanation in the Roman Catholic Church for the consecration of the elements of bread and wine, until its Aristotelian basis of 'substance' and 'accidents' was rejected as an outmoded philosophical explanation of matter.

This theory of anamnesis also shows how far liturgical theories have diverged from the gospel. As I mentioned earlier, the church had, through the centuries following the Enlightenment, voted for a pietistic and conservative, mediaeval understanding of Christian worship. This has remained true throughout the 20th century and remains the active understanding of worship in many parts of the church. Jesus and his sacrifice is past history, as Dix terms it. For many, the risen Lord does not appear to be, in practice, the one who calls us to worship but needs to be 're-called' into that worship so that we might effect, in ritual, the full benefits of salvation on behalf of the world.

If the reader has had patience to read this far, she or he may well be asking themselves, 'How can such things be? Is this what Christian worship is all about?' It is time to make the point that these 'anamnetic' theories of bringing back the past, or even the 'effects' of an event in the past, belong only to a pre-Enlightenment, mediaeval world of occult practices. The God I attempted to describe earlier on is the God whose 'character' is such that to provide liturgical 'miracles' is not compatible with his concern for the extending of his sovereignty in the world where truth can be seen as the initial response of humankind to the divine. The notion of bridging time so as to recover the effects of the 'saving events' of Jesus' death is mind boggling. But the idea that the pronunciation of a word, ('remembering'), in a rite is sufficient to 'achieve' this miracle is to treat God and the world as a convenience for maintaining orthodox doctrines against all common sense understanding. These notions are included in standard text books of liturgy and are taught to clergy throughout the world. None of the re-statements of eucharistic theology in the 20th century, either Catholic or reformed, has been able to cut loose from the mediaeval pre-occupation with the passion and death of Christ. In one form or another, the eucharist was said to be pleading the death of Christ before the Father. The New Testament has a different view of God. God is seen to be a participant with Christ in the redemption of us all. Paul writes in 2 Corinthians, 'God was in Christ reconciling the world to himself.'(2 Corinthians 5:19) As one writer has observed, if there was a sacrifice, it was made by God and not to God.[140] The deed was finished, once and for all. But for all who believe and who have died with Christ in baptism, a renewal of life is now possible - 'When anyone is united to Christ he is a new creature: his old life is over; a new life has already begun.'(2 Corinthians 5:17)

The anamnesis theory looks to find ways of connecting with the death. It has often been maintained by the 'anamnesis school' and others, that the letter to the Hebrews vindicates the idea that there is always a remembrance of the death of Jesus in the fact that he is said to be our intercessor in heaven. But the argument of Hebrews is that Jesus has superceded the Jewish high priestly role and as Son of God has been exalted to the right hand of God, where he is the forerunner of our race and is, consequently, if one needs to use the old nomenclature, a 'high priest',

> 'We have this as a sure and steadfast anchor of the soul, a hope that enters into the inner shrine behind the curtain, where Jesus has gone as a forerunner on our behalf, having become a high priest for ever after the order of Melchizedek ... "The Lord has sworn and will not change his mind, 'You are a priest for ever.'" This makes Jesus the surety of a better covenant. The former priests were many in number, because they were prevented by

---

[140] David Edwards in a recent article for the Modern Churchpersons Union.

death from continuing in office; but he holds his priesthood permanently, because he continues for ever. Consequently he is able for all time to save those who draw near to God through him, since he always lives to make intercession for them.' (Hebrews 7:17-25)

It has been assumed by many who wish to maintain an eternal atonement for sin before God, that this key text implies that the 'intercession' of Jesus as Son, is a 'pleading' of his death before God; but that is being read into the text. The Greek verb *entunchanein*, which is rare in the New Testament and which is translated 'intercession' in our English versions means, in general,

> 'meeting with a person or thing ... and in the present passage the idea is left in the most general form ... In the glorified humanity of the Son of man every true human wish finds perfect and prevailing expression.'[141]

Through the life, death and vindication of Jesus we are all enabled, as we 'turn' to God, to receive the free grace of love and forgiveness in union with the risen Lord present with and to us.

My hope is that in writing about these academic theories reason should be allowed its say and that a more truthful tradition may emerge. The tradition of the New Testament is clearly based on the person of Jesus present with us and to us in the world and in worship. One of the unusual problems for those who seek to 'bring into the present' the person of Christ and the effects of his passion is that while defining God as present, the risen Lord is obviously regarded as absent! Let us see if we can accept a presence of God and of Jesus which is in tune with both the New Testament evidence and also with reason, in the following section.

---

[141] B. F. Westcott, *Epistle to the Hebrews*, Macmillan, 1892, pages 191-192

Chapter 9

Presence

Presence of God

In the context of contemporary society in the West God is not believed to be a presence, but an absence. It is certainly true that this has happened over quite a long period of time. In fact, probably following the 18th century Enlightenment, when Europe was changing rapidly from an agricultural society to an urban one. From what I have said previously about the importance and vitality of the Enlightenment scholars, it is not their scepticism about the mediaeval outlook which was the cause of so much haemorrhages from the churches. The truth is probably nearer the fact, that at the time, both political and ecclesiastical powers were struggling to maintain the status quo. Both the Catholic and the Protestant arms of the church needed to cling to positions so recently won, for they feared that, (as it actually happened), atheistic doubts would cause shipwreck for Christian faith held in so straitjacket of a tradition. There was, and there still is, if my thesis is correct, a reluctance to change for the sake of truth. So how can we speak of the 'presence' of God today?

We have to acknowledge that this apparent absence of God is not a new fangled thing. From the first recorded writings, human society has never found it easy in practice to accustom itself to the rule of God. One of the factors in the situation has always been the necessity to fall back on rules made precisely to guard against 'atheism'. The Torah, and the taboos contained in many aspects of Hebrew life, were there precisely to hold before the woman or man the ineluctable aspects of living out one's life before the unseen deity. Judgement would befall the person who failed to maintain the aspect of a life lived in subservience to god in the smallest matters of religion and life. It is possible that we in the post modern world who have made such enormous strides in the control over our environment and in the problems facing us in daily life, are the first to be able to distance ourselves from the need others before us have felt of clinging to a god who demanded so much from us in an apparently negative way. We have, we feel, risen above that demand. But it is also true that the language of Christian faith does not seem able to connect with modern humans. It is a 'dead' language, and the language of the ghetto, even in books which set out to clarify the religious spirit for our times.

So presence of God, and relationship through religious rules, seem to be two sides of the 'god coin', at least in the history of religions. Now that we have overthrown the religious rules, God has 'disappeared'. Yet, today, philosophers continually debate and write about how God can relate to the world and the apportionment of his 'powers' in a modern, free society. It appears that, at a certain level, God will not go away! I have tried in an earlier chapter to argue for a god who, while being transcendent must also be in a personal relationship to us, at least if the idea of God is to be meaningful at all. Does this mean that an understanding of God present to us, must now be thought of only in personal, individualist terms - a modern equivalent of the pietistic movements of the past? A god who cannot be thought of as taking part in 'society' and who in the churches has become a god of the individual only? Certainly, as it has been noted, the aspect of church services, while still embracing the gatherings of worshippers, has become in many ways an appeal only to the individual. Yet the sense of the presence of God cannot be tied to our response or non response. One can surely set out a reasonable case for a god, who, if he 'exists', is the unseen presence with humanity. So bearing in mind the changes in our human situation as compared with the 'ages of faith', and the need for change in the attitude of church traditions, let us try.

When Jacob was on his journey to Paddan-aram he had a vision of the angels of God ascending and descending on a ladder set up on earth to heaven, and God stood above it. In the promise made by the Lord to Jacob, giving the land to him and his descendants, was the saying, 'Behold, I am with you ...' And in the morning Jacob set up a pillar and poured oil on the top of it as a vow that the place would be God's house if his journey should be successful. (Genesis 28:10-22) The idea that places where God had revealed himself should be 'holy' places has ever since, (and most surely goes back to pre-historic times), been the case. At least this was the case until the coming of Jesus. While the Second Temple in Jerusalem represented the dwelling place of God it was superseded by the claim of Jesus to the woman of Samaria,

> "Woman, believe me, the hour is coming when neither on this mountain nor in Jerusalem will you worship the Father. You worship what you do not know; we worship what we know, for salvation is from the Jews. But the hour is coming, and now is, when the true worshippers will worship the Father in spirit and truth, for such the Father seeks to worship him. (John 4:21-23)

According to Luke in Acts, the early disciples in Jerusalem still worshipped in the temple but also had their eucharistic meal in their own houses. However, after the destruction of the Temple, and always of course in the dispersion, the early Christian communities worshipped only in ordinary houses. Jesus, the risen Lord, present with them in their meals, was the presence of the holy. But by the middle of the 4th century, when larger places were required for the influx of people into the communities, basilicas were built, and particularly following the example of Constantine in his massive building programme of Christian churches in Jerusalem, Rome and Constantinople. Presumably on the model of pagan temples, these churches became set aside, consecrated places for Christian worship. Christian missions to the 'heathen' would always be accompanied by the re-consecration of temples and places for Christian worship.

Throughout the mediaeval period the 'sanctuary' of God was the holiest place on earth and one could flee to such places to seek asylum. It is perhaps the inheritance of such 'holy places' that has been the partial cause, at least in the past 400 years, of the lack of any sense of God's presence in the ordinary world. We know that the puritans tried very hard to eradicate the idea that churches were special holy places but the Restoration recovered the churches as consecrated places of worship. So throughout Christian history there has been this idea, which has a long pedigree, that God is almost 'confined' to consecrated buildings. At least, that has been the practical outcome. Piety, of course, flourished always, from the earliest Christian times, so that in their houses Christians would pray at regular times of the day and often keep the consecrated hosts in the early centuries to receive communion at home. There was always a sense in the early period, before the peace of Constantine, that the Christian community was actually separated off from the 'world' outside, which, given the experiences of paganism and the threat of persecution, was reasonable. It is too evident to say that this has all changed for the Western world. There may still be places where to be a Christian is a dangerous matter and therefore better to maintain a separation which somehow keeps God within the community.

Of course it is the experience of many people that at certain times in their lives they have been to a place - a church, or some other 'special' place - where they felt the sense of the 'other' and it has touched them and remained with them. They may not have associated that as a presence of the divine. The romantic poets of the 19th century, and others since then, have expressed their feelings about episodes in their lives -

'I have felt
A presence that disturbs me with the sense
Of elevated thoughts; a sense sublime
Of something far more deeply interfused
Whose dwelling is the light of setting suns,
And the round ocean, and the living air

> And the blue sky, and in the mind of man,
> A motion and a spirit, that impels
> All thinking things, all objects of all thought,
> And rolls through all things.[142]

Those lines from Wordsworth remind us that primarily, experience of the divine, however one might conceive of this 'other', requires a certain space, a pause from human activity and silence. That is true also between people. To be able to recognize the other there is often the need for a moment of recollection, the cessation of speech so that both may meet at the deepest level. From that experience one could then say that the recognition of the other is a form of love, a giving and a receiving, a going out of oneself to regain a sense of the other one would not normally achieve.

On the other hand, we are making the attempt to see whether it is possible to have a sense of the divine, a presence, within the boundaries and in the circumstances of ordinary daily living. Can we say that there is a presence of the transcendent God - creator, personal, gracious and free - among us, whether we acknowledge him or not? If he is all these things, then it must be true that whether we sense his presence or not, he is here. The only alternative is to deny his existence.

Part of the problem lies in the assumed stand-off between rational thought and pietism. (For the Christian believer, of course there is no conflict between these two attitudes; but we shall be coming to that shortly). Pietism would abstract from the details of daily life to 'realize' the presence of the divine because one believes. Rational thought, if acknowledging the existence of a sort of god I have outlined, might wish to say that God is present in such a way

---

[142] William Wordsworth, *Lines written a few miles above Tintern Abbey*, The Major Works, edited by Stephen Gill, Oxford World Classics, 2000, page 134.

that there is no need of pietism - a prayer or a meditation - in order to recognize the presence, at least in a general sense. Perhaps the most likely understanding will be the idea of Wordsworth that the 'other', the presence, is in the mind of man.[143] Here, where one seeks to be oneself in thought and feeling, is the opportunity for realization of the beyond and the within. Augustine, speculating on how we can know the image of God in the mind, understands the mind as a spiritual thing capable of knowing, loving and willing in itself and so Andrew Louth, commenting on Augustine's De Trinitate, X. xi.18-19, concludes that, according to Augustine,

> 'There is a completely co-equal trinity of memory, understanding, will in the mind, each member of the trinity entirely co-penetrates the others, there is complete co-inherence. So we have arrived at the true image of God in the mind ...'[144]

It has been part of the reason for this thesis that today we need to use our reason as part of our creative existence under, and beside, a transcendent creator who is with us in love and in sympathy with all our hopes. Presence of God, in other words, has to have a prior rational understanding. Pietism without understanding can be ephemeral or magical manipulation of a god of our own imagining. Feuerbach's strictures, which we mentioned before, then become true as we see God as the more than human being enlarged, a mirror image of ourselves, a projection of our own desires. A reasoned

---

[143]The idea that we have 'souls' is often rejected today in favour of the idea that we are perhaps better understood as 'spirited bodies', self-contained human beings without an additional immortal soul. See the study by Phillip Cary, *Augustine's Invention of the Self*, Oxford, New York, 2000; and Nancey Murphy, *Bodies and Souls, or Spirited Bodies?*, Cambridge, 2006.

[144] Andrew Louth, *The Origins of the Christian Mystical Tradition*, Clarendon, 1981, page 152.

belief in God can find support in the Hebrew scriptures and in the New Testament provided that what is found there is also under the control of reason so that we may be able to see a whole picture rather than a partial, pietistic revelation of the truth. On the whole the idea of God's presence to us can best be seen as the continual upholding presence of all that is. He is not to be seen as the interfering presence, for good or evil, in this or that event. The pre-Enlightenment, mediaeval outlook supported that sort of fairly unreasoned, magical approach. Today life can be seen - by the reality of faith in a God who is, and will be - as being enfolded by the holiness of the divine, drawing all things ultimately to perfection in the future. Human frailty remains; but if there is presence of God - if he is - then there is positive reason to go on believing in that presence.

Presence of Jesus the risen Lord

But now we need to move on to the idea of the presence of the risen Lord in the world and in Christian worship. I have already highlighted the importance of seeing Jesus as the risen Lord of the gospels, the sustained 'result' of the Father's joint work with the Jesus of the crucifixion in making a new creation open to all in Christ, 'not counting our trespasses.' So it is not only the presence of God enfolding all creation but also the risen Lord who, in the furtherance of the 'kingdom of God', is always present to us in the world. While Paul likened the church to the body of Christ, and so the church's presence in the world is a manifestation of Christ's presence, there is much more to the gospel than the secluding of Christ within the church. This is difficult for Christians to articulate when, above all, it is the 'absence' of God in the world which seems to be the controlling situation and hence the anonymity of Jesus as alive today. Christians in the West are, by and large, only two percent of the population and so their churches are seen rather as

Christian ghettoes in the midst of a seemingly alien and 'atheistic' world. So it is important for us to look at the New Testament accounts of the resurrection appearances and into the wider context of the claims of Christians that Jesus is alive.

In the first place, it is quite extraordinary, from a common-place, human point of view, to maintain that Jesus, who was a totally human personality, is alive today. The New Testament authors, however, maintain that he was 'raised', by God -

> 'This Jesus God raised up, and of that we all are witnesses.'(Acts 2:32)'; 'We were buried therefore with him by baptism into death, so that as Christ was raised from the dead by the glory of the Father, we too might walk in newness of life.' (Romans 6:4); 'And he died for all, that those who live might live no longer for themselves but for him who for their sake died and was raised.' (2 Corinthians 5:15); 'Through him you have confidence in God, who raised him from the dead and gave him glory, so that your faith and hope are in God.' (1 Peter 1:21)

There can be no doubt about their convictions, not only of Christ's resurrection but that we, who believe in him, are also to be taken into a new life now, as a foretaste of the life to come. These statements seem to suggest that the fact of the raising of Jesus had been taken in their stride. But from the gospel accounts of the appearances of the risen Christ we can see that on the contrary the original disciples had been startled almost out of their wits. At least the confusion in the various accounts of the appearances that had been handed down in the oral tradition seem to suggest that they did not at first know what to make of this extraordinary situation. In Luke's account of the walk to Emmaus, for instance, the two disciples are really nonplussed,

'That very day two of them were going to a village named Emmaus, about seven miles from Jerusalem, and talking with each other about all these things that had happened. While they were talking and discussing together, Jesus himself drew near and went with them. But their eyes were kept from recognizing him. And he said to them, "What is this conversation which you are holding with each other as you walk?" And they stood still, looking sad. Then one of them, named Cleopas, answered him, "Are you the only visitor to Jerusalem who does not know the things that have' happened there in these days?"' (Luke 24:13-18)

In Mark's account two women are told,

"Do not be amazed; you seek Jesus of Nazareth, who was crucified. He has risen, he is not here; see the place where they laid him. But go, tell his disciples and Peter that he is going before you to Galilee; there you will see him, as he told you." And they went out and fled from the tomb; for trembling and astonishment had come upon them; and they said nothing to any one, for they were afraid.' (Mark 16:6-8)

Whether there had been an ending to Mark's account, with some 'appearance' which has got lost, we shall never know. The gospel accounts are later than Paul's letters by a matter of twenty to thirty years and it is clear, from the variety and sometimes confusion, in the accounts, that the appearances recorded in these accounts are from a quite early period. Paul quoted from what had been handed down to him, 'that he was raised on the third day in accordance with the scriptures.' (1 Corinthians 15:4), followed by a summary of witnesses which doesn't tally at all points with the gospel appearances. We might also add that facts of the early Christians' witness to Jesus as the risen Lord are plain to see in the various theological accounts of the first three centuries, and most particularly in the courageous witness of martyrs in the sporadic persecutions.

Then, secondly, as a result of this vindication of Jesus as Lord, we see the gradual emergence of a 'church', a community of believers which by the fourth century was capable of being recognized as a public, 'world' movement. The tenacity to have arrived at that point, through the travail of sporadic persecution and martyrdom, needs something more than ordinary human inventiveness or wishful thinking - it has to be the result of a shared conviction of a new life beyond the possibilities ever envisaged before in society.

Following the appearances, it is only Luke in his account in Acts, who has Jesus 'taken up' after 40 days in an 'ascension' into heaven. While this device enabled him to mark the end of the appearances it also symbolically signified the glorification of Jesus who from that point on was 'with' the Father in heaven. This 'theological' conclusion has not really helped the later church to come to terms with the reality of the living Lord who, like the Father is not absent but 'present'. It has affected our understanding of worship, as we shall be seeing in the final chapters. Of course the 'presence' cannot be understood as the risen Lord 'at my elbow' as I type this. There has to be some form of theological and one might say philosophical understanding of the new age and the new relationship which was inaugurated when Christ was raised. So the later letter of Ephesians, (not generally thought to be by Paul), uses the phrase 'in the heavenly places' as a mode of expression,

> ' But God, who is rich in mercy, out of the great love with which he loved us, even when we were dead through our trespasses, made us alive together with Christ (by grace you have been saved), and raised us up with him, and made us sit with him in the heavenly places in Christ Jesus, that in the coming ages he might show the immeasurable riches of his grace in kindness

toward us in Christ Jesus.' (Ephesians 1:4-7)

There is not here a sense of a defining distinction now between 'earth' and 'heaven' - the three tiered cosmos has been radically changed. The New Testament authors made a quantum leap from the traditional view of heaven, earth and hell through their faith in the living Christ. The 'new Adam' had inaugurated the new age, in which, at the close of the age, at the parousia, he would be manifested, rather than 'coming again' from heaven.

> 'In the heavenly places ... has reference not to future blessings viewed as treasure stored up in heaven, but to benefits which belong to believers now. ... As in Colossians, it is made clear that the link with heaven is not one achieved by human techniques; it is through Christ. God has blessed believers with every spiritual blessing in the heavenlies in Christ.'[145]

Unfortunately, as the centuries went by, and probably by the fourth century, the old understanding of a three tiered universe returned - specifically as a Christian sort of spiritual geography. In the late middle ages this can be seen clearly in Dante's Divine Comedy with its Inferno, Purgatorio and Paradiso. There are theologies of worship today which, in principle, go back to the Ptolemaic universe, at odds with our common understanding of life.

In the biblical evidence for the presence of Jesus here and now there is the tacit assumption that despite the original 'unbelief' of the disciples when Jesus appeared to them, it will be believers to whom the possibility of a presence is vouchsafed. And this comes out clearly in Christian worship. But in the world today we have passed beyond the confines of religious separatism precisely because there

---

[145] Andrew T. Lincoln, *Paradise Now and Not Yet*, Cambridge, 1981, pages 141-142.

is so much agnosticism about Christianity. Faith in the risen Lord is indeed a necessity for going beyond agnosticism into both an affirmation of God and of what has been accomplished in Jesus. Yet, shorn of centuries' old traditions which may or may not speak to the individual today, the presence of Jesus as Lord may indeed come to people as he apparently came to the travellers to Emmaus. It will probably be, not in a religious form, but as truth, as the meaning of life. There is no longer any place for a dichotomy of faith and reasonable thought. Faith can come by understanding, to turn the aphorism (credo ut intelligam) round.

The Presence of Jesus in the Eucharist

We have seen that in the first two hundred years the eucharist was a celebration of praise and thanksgiving, seemingly unrelated to the canonical formula of Institution except in fragmentary form, as far as our sources go. It was a meal to which, like the last meal Jesus had, was added the remembrance of him in sharing the bread and the cup. There was, apparently, a great diversity in practice but the reason for the celebration was to participate in the risen life of the Lord, in his 'body' and 'blood'. Whatever else was added, of readings and prayers, the communion in the life of Jesus was paramount. But, as we shall be noting later, this communion was a sharing with the members, too. Jesus' life was the means of uniting the participants with one another. There was, at this time, no emphasis on the elements, on the consecrated bread and wine, for their own sake. The practice of taking some of the bread home to share in the communion during the week seemed to be a practice in some parts, particularly in North Africa, but there is no sense of the later ideas of 'holy things' apart from the use made in communion.

The eucharistic 'species', the bread and wine, were never linked in the New Testament to the actual body and blood of Jesus. When Jesus said, 'This is my body', he could not have made an identification with his flesh. The verb to be, used in this instance, does not make a direct material correspondence. As Xavier Léon-Dufour points out, quoting J. Dupont, '...the most natural meaning of the words over the bread would be: 'This signifies my body,' 'This represents my body.'[146] So Paul can say in the first letter to the Corinthians,

'The cup of blessing which we bless, is it not a participation in the blood of Christ? The bread which we break, is it not a participation in the body of Christ? Because there is one bread, we who are many are one body, for we all partake of the one bread.'(10:16-17)

The point that the bread and wine are not efficacious in themselves was also made by J. D. G. Dunn,

> '...the emphasis was not so much on what was eaten and drunk as on the sharing (koinōnia) of the same bread and cup (1 Cor 10:16) believers were one because they shared the same loaf (1 Cor 10:17) not because of some efficacy in the bread itself.'[147]

Dufour also goes on to consider the essential fact that the future meals will not have the limited function of the meal enabling them to be present at his death, but rather the new relationship between Jesus and the disciples. But Dufour goes on to assume that Jesus will be 'absent' from these future meals, '... not only will Jesus be the one who keeps his community alive, but the disciples and Jesus himself will become mysteriously one, despite the absence that must last as

---

[146] Xavier Léon-Dufour, *Sharing the Eucharistic Bread*, Paulist Press, New York, 1982, page 125.

[147] J. D. G. Dunn, *Unity and Diversity*, pages 164-5 .

long as the present world lasts.'[148] I would not only query the idea that the world is going to come (necessarily) to an end but also the statement that Jesus is not present at the meal. That is quite in tune with the traditional idea that the celebrant 'represents' Christ at the eucharist. It is one of the main points of my thesis that the Lord himself invites us to the eucharist and is present there as anywhere else. The philosophical question as to how God and the risen Lord can be present always to everyone and every place is not something that can be answered here (or perhaps at all!) One would like to change Dufour's comments on the bread, 'Paradoxically, for Jesus as for the believer, the eucharistic bread is and is not bread, it is and is not the body of Jesus.'[149], by saying that Jesus is present in faith and is not present in terms of physical materiality.

As we have seen previously, the communion with Jesus in the eucharist is called variously the 'flesh' or 'body' and the 'blood'. In Justin, who is writing probably about a hundred years after Paul, the bread and wine are eucharisticized by the words of thanks in the prayer of the president. So an 'effect' upon the elements is already showing itself by this time. Irenaeus also uses the word eucharisticize to denote the bread and the cup. But he introduces the word epiclesis, or 'invocation' as the mode of sanctification of the elements. Perhaps the phrase 'consecrated by the word of God' in 1 Timothy 4:4-5, 'For everything created by God is good, and nothing is to be rejected if it is received with thanksgiving; for then it is consecrated by the word of God and prayer', has some sort of parallel to Justin's statement, that the elements are consecrated 'through a word of prayer'. It is not clear that these second century authors knew of some liturgical rite of consecration, particularly as the words of the institution narrative do not seem to be used in this period. In any case, there does not seem to be any idea, that apart

---

[148] Dufour, page 69.

[149] ibid. page 128.

from the use of the elements, eucharisticized, for communion, that there was an actual 'change' in them. We have to wait until the late fourth century for an assertion of a specific, actual change in the elements which can either be by use of an invocation upon the elements or the use of the words of Christ in the narrative of the institution. The West used this latter form, which can be seen in Ambrose of Milan (339-397) in the late fourth century,

> 'By what words, then, is the consecration (effected), and by whose saying? (Those) of the Lord Jesus ...Christ's word accomplishes this sacrament.'[150]

It is important to note that in all discussion today about the presence of Jesus in the eucharist, it is often taken for granted that if Jesus is not substantially present in the bread and the wine, then the bread and wine only represent his presence symbolically.[151] That is commonly thought to be the truth of a protestant position by those who state their belief that there is a change in the elements brought about by the words of consecration. This is a false antithesis, as I have shown, because the Lord is always himself present in a transcendent presence. Sharing together in the bread and the wine we are joined in communion with the Lord and with each other. This is the reality of eucharistic communion which we need to recover and which I will argue for in the following section. We have also to ask ourselves regarding the idea of a consecration of the bread and wine into the body and blood of Jesus, whether this is commensurate with our understanding of God which we have attempted in an earlier section of this book. But apart from the use made by the West of the institution narrative in the late fourth

---

[150] Ambrose, *De Sacramentis* 4:14, in *Origins*, page 157.

[151] This is taken to be the historical position of Zwingli, opposed by other reformers of the 16th century.

century, the East, according to the sources we have from the fourth century, used the epiclesis as the form of consecration and we now need to look at the history and meaning of this idea.

CHAPTER 10

Epiclesis

While Irenaeus uses the word epiclesis, (used of the Holy Spirit, meaning 'to come upon'), at the end of the second century, we have just seen that this is a kind of parallel to the use of 'word' or logos that eucharisticizes the bread and wine for communion. The fully consecratory epiclesis at the end of the 4th century is explicit and quite distinct from these earlier usages of the word. So in the Mystagogical Catechesis ascribed to Cyril of Jerusalem, in the late 4th century, there is this comment,

> 'Next ... we call on the merciful God to send the Holy Spirit on those things that are being presented, so that he may make the bread Christ's body and the wine Christ's blood, for clearly whatever the Holy Spirit touches is sanctified and transformed.'[152]

The Liturgy of St John Chrysostom from the late fourth century, and still in use, has the following epiclesis,

> 'Again we offer you this spiritual and unbloody worship, and we ask and pray and beseech (you) send down your Holy Spirit upon us and upon these offered gifts, and make this bread the precious body of your Christ, changing (it) by your Holy Spirit, Amen!, and that which in this chalice the precious blood of your Christ, changing (it) by your Holy Spirit, Amen! ...'[153]

---

[152] Cited in *Origins*, page 148.

[153] In F. E. Brightman, *Liturgies Eastern and Western*, Oxford, 1896, page 329; quoted in Robert Taft SJ, *From logos to spirit; On the early history of the epiclesis*, in Hans-Jürgen Feulner et al. (eds), *Crossroad of Culture: Studies in Liturgy and Patristics in Honor of Gabriele Winkler*, Rome, 2000.

Epiclesis

We have already noticed that from the time of Justin onwards in the mid second century, there was realistic language about the flesh, or body and blood of Christ in connection with the bread and wine at eucharist. But these occurred not in actual forms of worship but in descriptions and commentaries and when actual text forms are discovered there is much more reticence, as in the Egyptian version of the anaphora of St Basil which prays,

> '... that in the good pleasure of your goodness your Holy Spirit may descend upon us and upon these gifts that have been set before you, and may sanctify them and show them as holy of holies.'[154]

Bradshaw has speculated that the genesis of particular invocations within the eucharistic prayer may have come from the use of the Aramaic acclamation marana tha, 'Our Lord, come!', which was used by Paul and which is also found in the Didache.[155] When it appeared that the eschaton, the final appearing of the Lord in glory was tarrying, so this became reflected in normal liturgical usages with an emphasis upon Jesus connected more closely with the eucharistic elements. So it is possible that the growth of a direct invocation upon the bread and wine in the first three centuries was descriptive while in the late fourth century it had become a theological necessity of the rite. But as Robert Taft has written, 'Its (epiclesis) prehistory, anterior to the earliest extant anaphoras (at the end of the fourth century on), is sheer speculation.'[156] There is also another twist to this history in that the institution narrative, previously used in catechetical lectures to give information about the

---

[154] In *Origins*, page 156.

[155] *Origins*, page 126.

[156] ibid. Taft.

origins of the eucharist in Jesus' words at the Last Supper was then apparently moved into the eucharistic prayer itself, but not necessarily as a 'consecratory' moment but for the same reason as formerly - to remind the congregation of the meaning of what was happening.[157]

By the late fourth century the eucharistic prayers were being written down. All that they contained had been 'sown' in the previous centuries, albeit with various and differing intentions. But it is clear that from this time there would be a more prominent emphasis on the eucharistic elements in themselves. Through John Chrysostom's preaching in Constantinople, for instance, there was already an added mystique, an element of what would later be introduced by Rudolph Otto as the *mysterium tremendum et fascinans* in respect of the 'fearful moment' of the consecration. And through his preaching apparently fewer people would be prepared to approach for communion. Bradshaw's thesis is relevant here,

> '... fourth century liturgical developments were often part of a process of disintegration of Christian worship rather than its full flowering. While it has been usual to view the elaborations of liturgical practice ... as manifesting the classic or golden age of liturgical evolution, in reality many of them are symptoms of a Church that was already losing the battle for the hearts and minds of its followers and was desperately trying to remedy the situation by whatever means lay to hand.'[158]

So we have to ask serious questions about this particular development of the 'conversion' of the bread and wine into the 'body' and 'blood' of Christ. The epiclesis in the East is one part of

---

[157] *Origins* page 140 ff.

[158] *Search*, page 218.

Epiclesis

this process. In the West it was the words of institution that were used to facilitate the conversion. The words of institution in the East perhaps remained catechetical and the epiclesis remained dominant. Today in the West the epiclesis has been re-inserted in the eucharistic prayer and it is followed by the institution which appears also to have still a consecratory role. So in Rite 2 of the Roman rite there is first of all the epiclesis,

> 'Lord, you are holy indeed, the fountain of all holiness. Let your Spirit come upon these gifts to make them holy, so that they may become for us the body and blood of our Lord, Jesus Christ',

followed later by the institution narrative.

The new eucharistic prayers of the Anglican church follow the same pattern with the epiclesis in a moderate, non-conversion form, in Prayer A,

> '... grant that by the power of your Holy Spirit these gifts of bread and wine may be to us his body and blood,'

followed by the institution narrative.

I am not concerned here with the details of any of the rites in use either in the Roman or Anglican rites or with any suggestions about them. I put them here as evidence of the logical conclusion of the process that began in the late fourth century. We need to be concerned whether this focussing on the elements reflects the actual reality of 'doing' the eucharist and is in reasonable accord with our view of ourselves and of the world as we know it today.

First of all in respect of what the transcendent, loving God can be asked to do in our liturgical services, is it actually possible for God, through Holy Spirit, to make a 'change' in the bread and wine? We are back to the idea of 'substantial forms' and 'real accidents' we enquired into in the first chapter.[159] Is the conversion of bread into the body of Jesus a specimen of the Aristotelian idea of 'action at a distance' or, as we might say, of 'remote control'? Remembering the discussion about God and of the possibility of his intervention into the world of human persons and events (see page 44), can we accept this automatic, non-personal, so-called sacramental activity? The Oxford English Dictionary notes that 'sacrament' is derived from Old French, *sacrement*, from the Latin, *sacramentum*, 'solemn oath', used in Christian Latin as a translation of the Greek mustērion, 'mystery'. In the New Testament the idea of 'mystery' is reserved for the understanding of God's secret which is to be revealed in Christ, for instance of the inclusion of the Gentiles, as in Ephesians 4:7-13.[160] So that while the word sacrament is derived from ancient pagan literature it does not mean for Christians the idea of a mysterious divine enactment on material things, as in the supposed change of bread and wine.[161]

We need to affirm that in Eucharist the bread is bread and that the wine is wine and not as Dufour so eloquently put it that it is bread and it is not bread. (See page 133) Jesus did not say that this will be changed into my body when you remember me. We have

---

[159] Descartes rejected the idea that matter was composed of substance and accidents and was therefore challenged by his critics to defend the scholastic view of the 'change' made in the bread and wine, the substance becoming the body of Jesus while the 'accidents' of bread remained. Descartes was a devout Catholic and did not wish to come into conflict with the ecclesiastical authorities. His reply was that the bread was *wholly* changed into the body of Jesus, with nothing remaining, but by divine arrangement we are convinced that the bread remains for us to see!

[160] See the extended note on *mustērion* in Armitage Robinson, *St Paul's Epistle to the Ephesians*, Macmillan, 1903, pages 234-240.

[161] Note also the mistaken understanding of 'mystery' in Odo Casel's view of liturgical action. (See page 115)

Epiclesis

seen that gradually, over three centuries, there came to be a change of focus in the eucharistic rites, in so far as they are able to be recognized from the sporadic accounts left to us. Since the mid twentieth century there has been a move to re-instate some of the late 4th century ideas because, it has been said, they are part of our catholic heritage. But do we need to do this? Above all, as this thesis maintains, it is the work of reason to have a share in our worship as Christians as well as in our ordinary life. And, as with the changing of water into wine, the changing of bread into the body of Jesus, besides being an anachronistic view of human substances, is to miss the whole point of Eucharist, as I shall point out. The anachronistic view belongs to the middle ages, having connections with magic, as with the alchemists search for the means with which to change lead into gold ingots. The New Testament view is one of divine and human relationships in Christ the Lord.

Jesus in his life-time drew around him a group of men (and we may also say women), who followed with him in his journeys to villages and towns. It was surely one of the aims in his life to leave behind him disciples, who would become a founding part of the kingdom of his Father which he had already inaugurated. At his death it seemed to the disciples that this would not happen. In fact they deserted, all of them, in the tragic circumstances of the trial and execution. But the night before he died he left them a symbolic meal, encapsulated in a meal: bread and wine taken and drunk in remembrance of him. He said, according to Mark's account, 'Take, this is my body.' It was the prophetic symbol of an actual relationship which they would know after his death and resurrection. It has often been speculated that the eucharistic meals which the disciples had after Easter were not only a throw back to the meals they had during the life and mission of Jesus - with all who wished to join in - but also that they were a direct result of the resurrection appearances, as at Emmaus and in Jerusalem, according to Luke. However that may be, the reality of the 'communion' meals that they enjoyed in Jerusalem after Easter were meals of the renewal of their relationship with Jesus, and in him with one another. The bread and wine being the human, and real, tokens of those events. So they continued these reunions with the risen Lord, as in the account in the Acts of the Apostles, which probably describes them:

> '... day by day, attending the temple together and breaking bread in their homes, they partook of food with glad and generous hearts, praising God ...' (Acts 2:46-47)

Secondly, it is important to make a bold move in all this history of eucharistic prayers, and to say that the understanding of eucharist from the very beginning was not of the details of the proper 'rite' and how to perform it, but that the entail of the institution of the eucharist made by Jesus before his death was an invitation offered by him to be with him. He would be the host in person at every gathering of Christians. In worship the living Christ is responded to - as the two women did when meeting him on the 'third day' -

> 'Mary Magdalene and the other Mary went to see the sepulchre ...And behold, Jesus met them and said, "Hail!" And they came up and took hold of his feet and worshipped him.' (Matthew 28:1-9)

The risen Lord is the host now at every celebration of the eucharist and the service of praise, thanksgiving and prayer is completed with the renewal of relationship in sharing the bread and wine. The divine one uniting himself with his friends.

CHAPTER 11

Worship as Believing - A Summary

We began by looking at the 16th-17th centuries explosion of thought in order that we might be able to have some base for my thesis that we need to use reason as well as revelation in our understanding of worship. The church, throughout the past four centuries, has found it hard to accept this, believing that what had been passed on in tradition from the early centuries could be accepted as the divine will for us whether it saw it in a catholic or an evangelical form.

Of course today science has long outstripped the tentative hypotheses of Descartes and others and philosophy has other matters to be engaged with in the 21st century, even if some still hold to Descartes 'dualism' of body and soul.[162] However, Descartes' proposal that we can come to belief in God through the exercise of our reason was quite in accord with the ideas of the scholasticism of his day. It was this which provoked the Protestant outcry that his ideas, without benefit of revelation, would lead to atheism. It is ironic that these ideas of the value of reason in the scholastic period, such as Aquinas and Descartes, can have approval in the post modern age! My brief outline of the new philosophy had the intention of encouraging the idea that to begin thinking along

---

[162] "The importance of Descartes' legacy to philosophy justifies the remarks of Kenny that: 'Those who accept a Cartesian view of the mind, I suppose, can admire Descartes for being the first to state truths with cogency and elegance and precision. But only one who is cured of Cartesianism can be fully awed by the breathtaking power of an intellect which could propagate, almost unaided, a myth which to this day has such a comprehensive grasp on the imagination of a large part of the human race.'" Quoted in Aristotle, De Anima, translated by Hugh Lawson-Tancred, Penguin, 1986, page 225, note 44. Quoted from C. Diamond and J. Teichman (eds), *Intention and Intentionality*, page 3.

reasonable lines when confronted with liturgical statements which seemed to belong to the law of the Medes and the Persians, was essential.

As I have tried to show, it is necessary to modify some of the ideas of God, such as omnipotence and omniscience, (also proposed in the revelation of the scriptures), by a reasoned, logical understanding more in accord with what we know of the world, ourselves and the cosmos today. The idea that we can know all that is to be known, for the purposes of Christian faith, from the Bible, has had a strong impetus in the past half century with the growth of fundamentalism, buttressed by the statement of the reformation that,

> 'Holy Scripture containeth all things necessary to salvation: so that whatsoever is not read therein, nor may be proved thereby, is not to be required of any man, that it should be believed an article of the Faith, or be thought requisite or necessary to salvation.'[163]

While this article proved a snare in the late 19th century to those who wished to believe in certain 'romish' practices, today it is a legal justification for those who wish to see scripture as the infallible, literal, inspired word of God. It does not need to be said that today, infallible ideas belong to another age, the age of the pre-Enlightenment.

The academic research of the past thirty years into the 'Jesus of history', which had in the previous century been almost abandoned for the moral and pedagogic Jesus, has shown that the gospel accounts of Jesus contain much more than that. Above all, as I have often emphasized, the gospel accounts intend to portray Jesus as the Jesus whom they know, the risen Lord, known by the early

---

[163] 39 Articles of the Church of England, Article VI.

Christian communities in their worship and for whom the gospel records were written. In this respect New Testament scholarship, while varying greatly in the conclusions individuals may reach, has at least given pointers to what seems to have been the reality of faith of the early disciples after Easter. Then Paul's own recognition and preaching of Jesus as the risen Lord, written at least 20 years previously, underpins this conclusion. This makes all the difference when one begins to try to speculate on the faith and practice of the early communities and, indeed for the next two centuries. The later theology based on the death and so-called atonement of Jesus can then be related, not to the root of Christian faith, but to the ideology of the times in which it appeared. As I have said, the penal substitution theory that Jesus died and suffered punishment instead of us is not to be found in the New Testament. Unfortunately it is widely believed to be true by biblicist Christians today. Certain phrases from the nineteenth century atonement theories, and the remodelling of atonement theories that has been taking place throughout the churches in ecumenical dialogue, have been retained in the renewal of eucharists that has taken place in the past half century and I have suggested that this is not in accord with either the New Testament understanding of the death of Jesus or our own reasonable, moral sensibilities.

Central also to my thesis is the concern that we should be able to recover the New Testament understanding that the risen Lord is present to us in a transcendent presence. He is not 'absent' in some other place such as a mediaeval 'heaven', but is the host at our eucharistic worship and present to the world. So the late fourth century theories, up to the present day, of how he is present in the species of bread and wine, become irrelevant. Concerning the 'change' either real or simply in the mind of the communicant, of the bread and wine into the body and blood of Jesus, we need to be clear that no such change is possible from our present understanding either of God or of the nature of bread and wine as substances, no matter how much tradition or practice is pleaded. Since the Reformation the Anglican church has always seen the solemn repetition of the words of Institution being the mode of consecration but without any theory of what was 'happening' at that moment in the service. But this left the understanding of what the eucharist meant hanging in the air! So the recent rehabilitation of the epiclesis in the new services has tried to address this point. But again we saw that the possibility of the Spirit being invoked to make 'changes' in the elements of bread and wine, either 'for us' or integrally in the elements, has no obvious link with our understanding of God in relation to us. Eucharistic theology remains today very much in the medieval domain of a concentration on the bread and wine as necessarily 'changed' either realistically or in the mind of the communicant. This conflicts with any understanding of matter in today's world or with our renewed ideas of God in relation to us and the world. It is in Christian worship that we are aware most particularly of the presence of the risen Lord and any 'reduction' of this relationship into a mode of ritual understanding is detrimental to the heart of that faith.

The eucharist, from the point of view of its origins, is a celebration of praise and joy in the presence of the risen Lord. The communion in the bread and wine is the actual renewal of relationship between the Lord and ourselves and with each other in him. Theology today needs to recover the sense of the constant relationship between the Lord and ourselves, the disciples. So in worship it is this relationship which is renewed and as one person has expressed it, 'It's the persons celebrating, not the bread and wine on the table [who are changed].' But the sharing in the one loaf is the expression of the reality of that relationship and it is in that relationship that the holiness of the rite of eucharist is expressed.

The simplicity of that ideal of eucharistic worship is difficult to encapsulate in a form of service. Part of the problem is that over the centuries the part played by the president, priest or minister has become fixed, whatever the theology of ministerial priesthood is in place. Again, this depends to a large extent on the size of the congregation. It is difficult to get away from the idea that what is being done is for the people rather by the people together. 'New presbyter is old priest writ large.' We need to recover the sense of the early Christian communities that the president is not one who stands in the place of Christ at the eucharist but is the enabler with the gathered community in the response of worship to God in Christ. Maybe it is a logistical problem. But to say that is to show how far we have departed from the understanding that Christian worship is the coming together of Christians in Christ before the Father in thanksgiving, and a participation in the new life in Christ and a re-commitment of discipleship. That could be seen as an attempt to return to the rather simple origins of the Christian communities; but like all things that mature it is impossible to go back to a supposedly idyllic age when everything was thought to be straightforward and clear. However that may be, the raison d'etre of worship remains to be implemented - viz. that worship is the response of faith to God in Christ. It is Worship as Believing.

It has been the underlying concern of this thesis that worship is not a rite to be performed so much as a response by those who come to worship the Father in the presence of the Lord and there to renew their commitment as disciples. So if there is anything in liturgy that is bound to a 'ritual' understanding, that is, to a rite that makes something 'happen', to change things, or tries to make present what has happened once for all in the past, then it is to that extent not of the Christian understanding of worship.[164] Ritual in

---

[164] A striking example of 'ritual' understanding occurs in David Torevell's book, *Losing the Sacred*, T&T Clark, 2000, pages 36-37.' Participants during a eucharist are not simply gathered around the sacrificial, saving victim on the altar, but share in his redemptive work by their physical and

(continued...)

that sense is about the god who is absent. But as I have tried to show, God for us is immanent and personal as well as transcendent in holiness. Jesus is not absent either. It is the mystery of a relationship with Christ that lies behind the whole tenor of the witness of the New Testament documents. In a wonderful and mysterious way Christ is present to all with a transcendent presence - 'he is Lord of all'. From the very beginning that is where eucharistic worship began - when Christ was made known in the breaking of the bread. Every eucharist is a proleptic experience of the Messianic Banquet when God shall be all in all.

---

[164](...continued)
mystical participation *in his body*. They *become his body* ... The corporeal transformations which take place concerning the body of Jesus, become responsible, in the words of Ward, for an 'ontological scandal' since time and space are redefined to accompany the varied transpositions of Jesus' physical body ... :Liturgical and ritualized spaces are particularly sacred because they are often the most concentrated areas for the presence of such transpositions of the body of Jesus ... The church enacts and is united with Christ ... by making present throughout the liturgical year those things which the body of Christ endured itself when constituted as a physical male form ... it becomes the new yet same broken body of Christ, distributed for the salvation of the world.' (The author's emphasis)

Bibliography

Augustine. *Confessions*, transl R. S. Pine-Coffin, Penguin, 1961.
Barclay, John and Sweet, John, eds. *Early Christian Thought in its Jewish Context*, Cambridge, 1996.
Bedale, S. *The Eucharistic Sacrifice*, Theology, lvi, No. 398, 1953.
Boswell. *Life of Johnson*, ed. G. B. Hill, Oxford,1887; quoted in Woolhouse, The Empiricists, Oxford, 1998.
Bradshaw, Paul. F. *The Search for the Origins of Christian Worship*, 2nd Edition, SPCK, 2002.
---------------------- *Eucharistic Origins*, SPCK, 2004.
Brown, Driver & Briggs. *Hebrew & English Lexicon*, Oxford, 1906.
Brunner, Emil. *Revelation & Reason*, transl. Olive Wyon, SCM, 1947.
Carpenter, S. C . *Church & People*, 1789-1889, Part 1, SPCK, 1959.
Cary, Phillip. *Augustine's Invention of the Self*, Oxford, New York, 2000.
Chadwick, Owen. *The Victorian Church*, Parts I & II, Adam & Charles Black, 1972.
---------------------- *The Mind of the Oxford Movement*, Adam & Charles Black, 1960.
Clarke, Desmond M.. (1998), *Descartes*, Penguin.
Coakley, Sarah and Pailin, David A., (eds.) *The Making and Remaking of Christian Doctrine*, Oxford, 1933.
Cottingham, John. *Descartes*, Blackwell, 1988.
---------------------- *The Rationalists*, Oxford, 1988.
---------------------- *The Spiritual Dimension*, Cambridge, 2005.
Creighton, Mrs Mandell. *Life and Letters of Mandell Creighton*, Longmans Green, 1906.
Curley, M., *The Collected Works of Spinoza, Ethics*, Princeton, 1985
Davies, D. R. *Paul & Rabbinic Judaism*, SPCK, 1955.
Davies, Brian and Leftow, Brian, *The Cambridge Companion to ANSELM*, Cambridge, 2004.
Descartes, René. *The Principles of Philosophy*, transl Desmond M. Clarke, Penguin, 1998.

Dix, Gregory. *The Shape of the Liturgy*, Dacre Press, 1945.
Dunn, J. G. D. *Unity & Diversity in the New Testament*, SCM, 1977.
Elliott-Binns, L. E. *Religion in the Victorian Era*, Lutterworth, 1966.
Evans, C. F. *Luke*, SCM, 1990.
Fenwick, John & Spinks, Bryan. *Worship in Transition*, T & T Clark, 1995.
Feuerbach, Ludwig. *The Essence of Christianity*, transl George Eliot, Prometheus, New York, 1989.
Gilkey, L. B. *Naming the Whirlwind*, Indianapolis, Bobb-Merrill, 1969.
Grey, Buchanan. *Sacrifice in the Old Testament*, quoted in Jones, JTS, N. S. Vol. VI, Pt 2, 1955.
Guiver, George. *Company of Voices*, SPCK, 1988.
Hermas, *Similitudes*, in Lightfoot, The Apostolic Fathers, Macmillan, 1898.
Hooker, Morna D. *Not Ashamed of the Gospel*, Paternoster Press, 1994.
Hughes, Graham, *Worship as Meaning*, Cambridge, 2000.
Hume, David. (1777), *An Essay Concerning Human Understanding*, Oxford Philosophical texts, edited by Tom L. Beauchamp, Oxford 1999
Irenaeus. *Adv. Haer*. In Henry Bettenson, Documents of the Christian Church, Oxford, 1943.
Israel, Jonathan I. *Radical Enlightenment*, Oxford, 2002.
Jeremias, J. *The Eucharistic Words of Jesus*, SCM, 1966.
Jones, C. P. M., Wainwright, G., Yarnold, E. SJ, Editors: *The Study of Liturgy*, SPCK, 1978.
Jones, D. R., Journal of Theological Studies, New Series Vol. VI, part 2, October, 1955.
Léon-Dufour, Xavier. *Sharing the Eucharistic Bread*, transl Matthew, J. O'Connell, Paulist Press, New York, 1982.
Lincoln, Andrew. *Paradise Now & Not Yet*, Cambridge, 1981.
Lindars, Barnabas. *The Gospel of John*,

New Century Bible Commentary, Eerdmans, 1972

Locke, John. *An Essay in Human Understanding*, (ed.) Roger Woolhouse, Penguin, 1997.

Louth, Andrew. *The Origins of the Christian Mystical Tradition*, Clarendon, 1981

Käsemann, Ernst. *Essays on New Testament Themes*, SCM, Studies in Biblical Theology, No. 41, 1964.

McGowan, Andrew. *Ascetic Eucharists*, Oxford, 1998.

Moule, C. F. D. *Forgiveness & Reconciliation*, SPCK, 1998.

Mozley, J. K. *The Doctrine of the Atonement*, Duckworth, 1953.

Murphy, Nancey. *Bodies and Souls, or Spirited Bodies?*, Cambridge, 2006

Newton, Isaac. (1687) Newton, *Philosophical Writings*, Andrew Janiak (ed.), Cambridge, 2004.

Otto, Rudolph. *The Idea of the Holy*, Pelican, 1959.

Pailin, David A. *God and the Processes of Reality*, Routledge, 1989.

---------------------- *Probing the Foundations*, Pharos, 1994.

---------------------- *The Anthropological Character of Theology*, Cambridge, 1990.

Pascal, Blaise. *Pensées*, translated A. J. Krailsheimer, Penguin, 1966.

Roberts & Donaldson. *The Ante-Nicene Fathers*, Vol. 1, Eerdmans, 1884.

Robinson, Armitage, *St Paul's Epistle to the Ephesians*, Macmillan, 1903.

Sanders, E. P. *Paul & Palestinian Judaism*, SCM, 1977

Spinoza, B., *A Theologico-Political Treatise*, (Transl.) R. H. M. Elwes, Dover Publications, 2004.

Stevenson, J. *A New Eusebius*, SPCK, 1974.

Stone, Darwell. *A Study of the Doctrine of the Holy Eucharist*, Longmans, 1909.

Temple, William. *Christus Veritas*, Macmillan, 1930.

The Later Christian Fathers, transl. and edited by Henry Bettenson, Oxford, 1970.

Torevell, David. *Losing the Sacred*, T & T Clark, 2000.

Viney, D. W., *Charles Hartshorne and the Existence of God*, State University of New York, Albany, 1985

Vidler Alec. *The Church in an Age of Revolution*, Penguin, 1961.

Westcott, B. F. *The Epistle to the Hebrews*, MacMillan, 1892.

Woolhouse, R. S. *The Empiricists*, (1988), A History of Western Philosophy:5, Oxford

Wordsworth, William. *The Major Works*, edited Stephen Gill, Oxford, 2000.

Wright, N. T. *Jesus and the Victory of God*, SPCK, 1996.

Index

1662 Book of Common Prayer 29, 38, 87
1928 Prayer Book 67
39 Articles 38, 40, 86, 144
anamnesis 36, 106, 110-118
Anselm 42, 84-86, 102, 149
Antioch 93, 96
Aristotle 2, 143
Athanasian 61
Augustine 42, 84, 104, 126, 149
Bacon 3, 4
Barth 35
Berkeley 14, 15
bread 22, 28, 74, 80, 87, 91-98, 100, 108, 114, 116, 117, 132-140, 139-142, 145, 146, 148, 150
Brunner 35, 36, 149
catechesis 91, 100, 136
Chalcedon 60, 61
Chrysostom 100, 136
Constantinople 100, 123, 138
Cottingham 6, 7, 9, 149
Cur deus homo 85, 86
Cyprian 83, 96, 98, 99, 109
Cyril of Jerusalem 68, 99, 136
Darwin 34
death of Christ 78, 79, 81, 84, 90, 94, 100, 118
deism iv, 36
Descartes 2, 5-10, 12, 13, 15-17, 139, 143, 149
Didache 91, 94, 95, 101, 137
Dix 110, 111, 113, 116, 117, 150
epiclesis iv, v, 134-139, 146
eucharistic prayer 100, 137, 138

evangelical iv, 22, 23, 25, 70, 143
expiation 71, 80, 100
faith 1-iii, 15, 23, 26, 30, 32, 34, 38, 39, 41, 54, 55, 59, 69, 80, 83, 89, 104, 105, 121, 122, 127, 128, 130, 131, 134, 144-147
Gassendi 10
heaven 1, 2, 24, 43, 59, 109, 118, 122, 130, 131
Hobbes 10
Hume 13, 33, 37, 150
immanence 44
institution narrative 80, 90, 101, 134, 135, 137, 139
Irenaeus 83, 84, 97-99, 101, 113, 134, 136, 150
Jesus iv, 20, 28, 35-37, 45-48, 51, 54, 55, 58-66, 69-84, 87-98, 100-106, 108, 109, 113, 115-119, 123, 127-135, 137, 139-142, 144, 145, 147, 148, 150, 152
Justin 90, 96-98, 101, 113, 134, 136
Kant 13, 17
kingdom of God 37, 64, 72-74, 76, 77, 79, 92, 104
Last Supper 74, 75, 80, 90, 91, 93, 137
Laud 19
Leibniz 12-14, 53
Liturgical Move. iv, 29, 30, 67

Locke 13, 32, 150
Maurist 68
memory 7, 15, 51, 74, 99, 106-109, 126
miracles 1, 11, 33, 35, 37, 45-48
Moule 65, 66, 151
Newman 26
Newton 4, 5, 14, 53, 151
Nicea 59, 60
omnipotence 41, 62, 144
omniscience 41, 62, 144
Origen 84
Otto 43, 44, 138, 151
Oxford Movement 24, 26, 149
Pailin 50, 53, 61, 89, 149, 151
Pascal 52, 54, 151
Paul 47, 48, 51, 52, 58, 60, 61, 65, 68, 69, 71, 74, 77-82, 88, 90, 91, 93, 98, 99, 102, 109, 114, 118, 127, 129, 130, 132, 134, 137, 149, 151
presence iv, 28, 36, 38, 65, 66, 70, 104, 108, 115, 119, 121-127, 131, 132, 135, 145-148
president 97, 134, 146, 147
priest 10, 98, 99, 118, 146, 147
Pusey 28
ransom 22, 24, 76
redemption 71, 80, 87, 100, 118
remembrance iv, 70, 90, 92, 93, 97, 98, 101, 106, 108, 110, 111, 113, 115, 118, 132, 141
resurrection 47-49, 58, 60, 79-81, 83, 84, 98, 104, 111, 127, 128, 141
revelation iv, 9, 15, 16, 30, 32, 35-37, 40, 54, 61, 127, 143, 144, 149
Rome 26, 28, 96, 97, 99, 123, 136
sacrifice 71, 78, 80, 83, 84, 87, 95, 96, 98-100, 102, 104, 111, 113, 116-118, 149, 150
Sanders 71, 81, 103, 151
Sellon 28
Spinoza 10-14, 16, 33, 34, 37, 149, 151
substance 3, 8, 12, 60, 106, 139
substitution 71, 145
Syria 91, 93
temple 62, 63, 65, 66, 75, 123, 141, 151
Temple, William 57, 151
water 46, 96, 97, 141
Wesley 20-22, 24
Westcott 32, 112, 119, 152
Whitehead 89
Wilberforce 23
wine 22, 28, 46, 87, 96, 97, 106, 116, 117, 132-142, 145, 146
Wordsworth 27, 125, 126, 152
Wright 37, 76, 77, 152

ISBN 1425121454